Saara Idelbi is ranked as a leading junior in Administrative and Human Rights Law in the Legal 500, and specialises in claims human rights, equality, and judicial review claims. She speaks regularly on her areas of expertise.

Saara holds a Masters in Public Law and Human Rights, worked as judicial assistant in the UK and South Africa, and is an Advocacy Trainer at Gray's Inn. She is appointed to the EHRC's and Attorney General's B Panels, and is a Fee-Paid First Tier Tribunal Judge in the Health and Social Entitlement Chambers. Saara practises from 5 Essex Chambers.

Paige Jones is a barrister at 5 Essex Chambers practising in public law and regularly deals with civil disputes between individuals and State authorities. Paige has a Master's degree in International Human Rights Law and has worked with international development organisations and domestic charities on rights-based issues.

A Practical Guide to Non-Pecuniary Damages in Human Rights Act Claims

A Practical Guide to Non-Pecuniary Damages in Human Rights Act Claims

Saara Idelbi
Barrister, Gray's Inn
LLB (Hons), LLM

Paige Jones
Barrister, Inner Temple
LLB (Hons), LLM

Law Brief Publishing

Published 2024 by Law Brief Publishing, an imprint of Law Brief Publishing Ltd
30 The Parks
Minehead
Somerset
TA24 8BT

www.lawbriefpublishing.com

Paperback: 978-1-914608-45-2

For my family, who teach me every day how to listen for more than just words, and to my husband, who supports me, proof-reads, and makes a mean grilled cheese.

– Saara Idelbi

For my Mum and Dad, who have always given me their unwavering support.

– Paige Jones

PREFACE

Lawyers across the country who advise their clients in relation to Human Rights Act claims are regularly faced with the task of undertaking extensive legal research in order to properly advise their clients on the difficult question of quantum.

About seven years ago, I remember being told that the sum, generally pitched, for damages in Human Rights Act claims was around £10,000. As time went on, it was inevitable that that general approach could not be viable.

This book reveals that £10,000 as an award could be excessive or wholly deficient, depending on the circumstances. When one starts looking into non-pecuniary damages in Human Rights Act claims, there is no paucity of criticism of the Strasbourg case law's apparent lack of cohesion or discernible legal principles. Is it too optimistic to conclude that that is, in itself, the applicable principle? Just satisfaction is human and not legal; seeking fixed patterns of just satisfaction is as futile as seeking fixed patterns in human behaviour. Perhaps it is.

Whilst the academic and legal debate continues, this book brings together in one place the data points (the case law), where awards for non-pecuniary damage have been made, for legal practitioners to consider what pattern may exist and/or how those data points assist you in your cases.

The research that underpins this book is up to date as at 30th September 2024. It details many, if not all, the relevant domestic cases at the time of publication where non-pecuniary damages have been awarded, and many of the cases from the European Court of Human Rights. This book will summarise the general principles before reviewing the cases in respect of individual articles (though cases involving Article 14 are dealt with in the engaged Article chapter). We hope that this book has the impact of saving practitioners' time and acts a handy guide to navigating quantum in Human Rights Act claims.

We are grateful to Law Brief Publishing for the opportunity to publish this book, and for the team's patience in our getting it over the finishing line. Thank you to our friends, Caroline, Matt and Jack, for their generosity and keen eyes.

Most of all, from me, thank you to Paige.

Saara Idelbi
October 2024

CONTENTS

Chapter One	Introduction	1
Chapter Two	General Principles	7
	Approach Principles	8
	Calculation Principles	19
Chapter Three	Articles 2 and 3	25
	Introduction and Principles	26
	Detention	29
	Criminal Justice	35
	Social Services	41
	Immigration	44
Chapter Four	Article 4	47
	Introduction and Principles	47
	No Award	49
	Awards for Violations of Article 4 and Other Articles	51
	Article 4 Alone	54
Chapter Five	Article 5	63
	Introduction and Principles	64
	Parole	66
	Detention Following Arrest	76
	Mentally Disordered	78

	Committal	83
	Military Custody	86
	Immigration	87
Chapter Six	Article 6	93
	Introduction	94
	Criminal Proceedings	95
	Civil Proceedings	98
	Family Proceedings	99
Chapter Seven	Article 7	109
	Introduction	109
	No Award	110
	Article 7 Alone	110
	Awards for Violations of Article 7 and Other Articles	112
Chapter Eight	Article 8	117
	Introduction	117
	Immigration	118
	Housing and Home	123
	Employment	131
	Family and Relationships	132
	Welfare Benefits	143
	Healthcare	144
	Criminal Justice	147
	Prisons	154

	Surveillance	160
	Privacy and Use of Private Information	165
	Article 8 and Article 10 and Misuse of Private Information	169
Chapter Nine	Article 9	177
	Introduction	177
	United Kingdom	178
	Other States	179
Chapter Ten	Article 10	183
	Introduction	183
	Journalism	184
	Protest	189
Chapter Eleven	Article 11	191
	Introduction	191
	United Kingdom	192
	Other States	193
Chapter Twelve	Article 12	195
	Introduction	195
	United Kingdom	196
	Other States	196
Conclusion		199

CHAPTER ONE

INTRODUCTION

1. The monetisation of rights, or indeed the quantification of when a right has been breached, can feel an uncomfortable exercise to some. To others, damages as just satisfaction for the breach of a right/s is a natural consequence; compensation as vindication is common in the English and Welsh legal system. The conflicting views, and all that exists in between, has attracted much debate, but you will not find that here. This is a practical guide for the calculation of non-pecuniary damages in claims under the Human Rights Act 1998 ("**HRA**") for breaches of articles of the European Convention on Human Rights and Fundamental Freedoms ("**Convention**"), in Schedule 1 of the HRA. It is what exists now, rather than why it exists.

2. Article 41 of the Convention states:

   "If the Court finds that there has been a violation of the Convention or the Protocols thereto, and if the internal law of the High Contracting Party concerned allows only partial reparation to be made, the Court shall, if necessary, afford just satisfaction to the injured party."

3. Section 8 HRA sets out judicial remedies in the following terms:

   "(1) In relation to any act (or proposed act) of a public authority which the court finds is (or would be) unlawful, it may grant such relief or remedy, or make such order, within its powers as it considers just and appropriate.

   (2) But damages may be awarded only by a court which has power to award damages, or to order the payment of compensation, in civil proceedings.

(3) No award of damages is to be made unless, taking account of all the circumstances of the case, including—

(a) any other relief or remedy granted, or order made, in relation to the act in question (by that or any other court), and

(b) the consequences of any decision (of that or any other court) in respect of that act, the court is satisfied that the award is necessary to afford just satisfaction to the person in whose favour it is made.

(4) In determining—

(a) whether to award damages, or

(b) the amount of an award,

the court must take into account the principles applied by the European Court of Human Rights in relation to the award of compensation under Article 41 of the Convention…."

4. Just satisfaction may be achieved simply by the finding of a violation or a declaration.[1] Section 8(3) HRA reflects that possibility. In reality, and generally, the request for an award of damages in HRA claims is effectively the default starting point. Crude though it may be, the top and bottom line of a claim remains the money. Where parties are encouraged to resolve cases early,[2] and where the time and financial costs of proceedings can outstrip awards for damages made under the HRA, estimating the best and worst case scenarios for damages is vital.

---

1 Paragraph 4 of the ECtHR's Practice Direction on Justice Satisfaction.

2 The Overriding Objective in the Civil Procedure Rules.

5. Though damages have been awarded both by domestic courts ("**courts**") and the European Court of Human Rights ("**ECtHR**") for many years, calculating an award for non-pecuniary damage that affords just satisfaction is challenged by conceptual difficulties in how ECtHR has decided the value of the awards made, with the ECtHR adjusting awards by reference to the respondent government against whom such an award is made.[3] The instinctive approach to damages is germinated in our domestic legal education. The reflex approach to calculating quantum under the HRA by applying domestic law is tempting, but such an approach has the potential to: become frustratingly circular, in that the domestic application of section 8(4) HRA requires the courts to look to the principles applied by the ECtHR; be contradictory, in that in the domestic context damages are awarded as a standard whereas section 8(3) HRA suggests that one progresses through other methods to achieve just satisfaction before reaching the question of damages at all; and/or is inconsistent with the reminders that the courts have given, i.e. that the HRA (and damages made pursuant to it) are not the same as a tort statute, has a different purpose and/or to align the domestic and Convention approach would be a fallacy.

6. If you have decided to pick up this book, you probably already understand the practical reality of calculating damages to achieve "just satisfaction". Settling on what figure is not a straightforward exercise, more often than not. Lord Bingham in *R (Greenfield) v Secretary of State for the Home Department* [2005] UKHL 14 observed:[4]

3 Paragraph 14 of the ECtHR's Practice Direction on Justice Satisfaction; *R (KB) v Mental Health Appeal Tribunal* [2003] EWHC 193 (Admin) at [23].

4 At [7B].

> "There is a risk of error if Strasbourg decisions given in relation to one article of the Convention are read across as applicable to another."

7. Similarly, there is a risk of error if awards in respect of a type of conduct under one article are read across as applicable to all types of conduct within the same article. This guide aims to mitigate those risks by looking at, in each chapter, the principles from the ECtHR in respect of particular articles (or within the particular article) and the application of the principles of particular articles in the courts. But, this is not just a book of quantum reports. It is intended to aid in understanding what just satisfaction looks like in monetary terms.

8. In *R (Sturnham) v Parole Board and another (Nos 1 and 2)* [2013] UKSC 23 at [29], Lord Reed JSC stated:

> "… the primary source of the principles which are to guide the courts in its application is said to be the practice of the international court that is its native habitat. I would however observe that over time, and as the practice of the European court comes increasingly to be absorbed into our own case law through judgments such as this, the remedy should become naturalised. While it will remain necessary to ensure that our law does not fall short of Convention standards, we should have confidence in our own case law under section 8 once it has developed sufficiently, and not be perpetually looking to the case law of an international court as our primary source."

9. As a consequence, having confidence in the awards made in the UK, where there have been many cases in the UK where non-pecuniary damages have been awarded, this book will focus on UK cases.

10. Where there are limited cases decided by UK courts in which non-pecuniary damages were awarded, then this book will focus on cases from ECtHR concerning the UK, and then, in the limited

circumstances where there are few representative cases concerning the UK, this book will look at cases from the top five largest economies in Europe by GDP (excluding the UK, which – at the date of writing – was one of the top five largest economies in Europe by GDP) to focus on awards where there is a comparable cost of living[5] taking into account "local economic circumstances in the Respondent States in its calculations."[6]

11. The ECtHR cases concerning the United Kingdom appear first in order, regardless of date, followed by other states. The ECtHR's Practice Direction also takes into account whether there have been several violations of protected rights by a particular respondent state,[7] and awards against a particular respondent state may be skewed by the frequency with which awards had been made against that particular state in the particular period of time so should be treated with caution.

12. Where the award made by the ECtHR is in euros, this book will specify the exchange rate at the time of the award by reference to the ONS's calculation of the average sterling exchange rate for euros,[8] but does not calculate inflation as, by the time this book may be read, the impact of inflation may have changed. The dates of the decisions have been included to assist you in calculating inflation.

13. The Convention is a living instrument and will continue to be interpreted in light of the presenting conditions at the time a case is

---

5 *R (Sturnham) v Parole Board and another (Nos 1 and 2)* [2013] UKSC 23 at [38].

6 Paragraph 14 of the ECtHR's Practice Direction on Just Satisfaction.

7 Paragraph 13 of the ECtHR's Practice Direction on Just Satisfaction.

8 https://www.ons.gov.uk/economy/nationalaccounts/balanceofpayments/timeseries/thap/mret.

decided.[9] Practitioners must be mindful of whether and how the interpretation of the living instrument may have changed.

---

9 *Tyrer v the United Kingdom* (1979-80) 2 E.H.R.R. 1.

CHAPTER TWO

GENERAL PRINCIPLES

1. Section 2(1) HRA obliges a court or tribunal, determining a question which has arisen in connection with a Convention right, to take into account any judgment, decision, declaration or advisory opinion of the ECtHR. It has been observed that there is a subtle difference in the wording of section 2(1) HRA and that of section 8(4) HRA, suggesting that Parliament intended that the courts have greater freedom on the amount of damages awarded.[10] However, the instruction came that the making and valuation of non-pecuniary damages for the violation of a Convention right required the courts to take into account the ECtHR jurisprudence. In *R (Greenfield) v Secretary of State for the Home Department* [2005] UKHL 14 ("***Greenfield***"), Lord Bingham confirmed that "*[it] is…to Strasbourg that British courts must look for guidance on the award of damages.*"[11] Accordingly, the domestic courts ought to follow "*clear and constant jurisprudence*" in the absence of some special circumstances[12] (the mirror approach[13]), but are not strictly bound by ECtHR jurisprudence.[14]

---

10 *R (KB) v Mental Health Appeal Tribunal* [2003] EWHC 193 (Admin) at [22].

11 At [6].

12 *R (Alconbury Developments Ltd) v Secretary of State for the Environment, Transport and the Regions* [2001] UKHL 23 at [26]

13 Edelman et al. (Ed), *McGregor on Damages* (22nd Edition, Sweet & Maxwell, 2024) 51-000; J Varuhas, *Damages and Human Rights*, Hart Publishing, 2018, at [230].

14 *R (Sturnham) v Parole Board* [2013] UKSC 23 at [27].

2. This chapter looks at the principles in two stages:

   a. Whether non-pecuniary damages should be awarded at all – "Approach Principles"; and, if so,

   b. What factors should be considered in determining the level of the monetary award – "Calculation Principles".

Approach principles

The purpose of an award

3. The courts have repeatedly stated that the objective of remedies in human rights claims is different to the objective in domestic private law claims.

4. In *Anufrijeva v London Borough of Southwark and others* [2003] EWCA Civ 1406 ("***Anufrijeva***"), Lord Woolf CJ explained that:

> "Where an infringement of an individual's human rights has occurred, the concern will usually be to bring the infringement to an end and any question of compensation will be of secondary, if any, importance. This is reflected in the fact that, when it is necessary to resort to the courts to uphold and protect human rights, the remedies that are most frequently sought are the orders which are the descendants of the historic prerogative orders or declaratory judgments... None of the convention rights in Section 1 of the Convention is of such a nature that its infringement will automatically give rise to damage that can be quantified in financial terms...The primary object of the proceedings will often be to bring the adverse treatment to an end."[15]

[15] At [53] and [60].

5. Similarly, in *Greenfield*, Lord Bingham said:

> "the focus of the Convention is still on securing observance by member states of minimum standards in the protection of the human rights specified in the Convention...the 1998 Act is not a tort statute. Its objects are different and broader. Even in a case where a finding of violation is not judged to afford the applicant just satisfaction, such a finding will be an important part of his remedy and an important vindication of the right he has asserted. Damages need not ordinarily be awarded to encourage high standards of compliance by member states, ... the purpose of incorporating the Convention in domestic law through the 1998 Act was not to give victims better remedies at home than they could recover in Strasbourg but to give them the same remedies without the delay and expense of resort to Strasbourg."[16]

6. Lord Brown in *Van Colle v Chief Constable of the Hertfordshire Police* [2008] UKHL 50 at [138], reiterated that claims under the HRA 1998 have a different purpose to those in common law:

> "Convention claims have very different objectives from civil actions. Where civil claims are designed essentially to compensate claimants for their losses, Convention claims are intended rather to uphold minimum human rights standards and to vindicate those rights. That is why time limits are markedly shorter . . . It is also why section 8(3) of the [HRA] provides that no damages are to be awarded unless necessary for just satisfaction."

7. In *Commissioner of Police of the Metropolis v DSD* [2018] UKSC 11, Lord Kerr repeated Lord Brown's observations. He stated at [65]:

---

16 At [4] and [19].

> "Laws LJ said in para 68 of his judgment in the Court of Appeal [2016] QB 161, that the inquiry into compliance with the article 3 duty is first and foremost concerned, not with the effect on the claimant, but with the overall nature of the investigative steps to be taken by the state. I agree with that. The award of compensation is geared principally to the upholding of standards concerning the discharge of the state's duty to conduct proper investigations into criminal conduct which falls foul of article 3. In paras 72—77 of his judgment, Laws LJ set out the systemic and operational failures of the appellant, quoting extensively from the judgment of Green J as to the first of these. That catalogue of failures was considered to warrant the award of compensation to the respondents…"

8. Indeed, at the same time the line of cases in the senior courts in England and Wales were opining on the purpose of monetary awards in HRA claims, the Grand Chamber in ECtHR stated, in *Varnava and others v Turkey* (Application nos. 16064/90 and others, 18 September 2009) at [224], that:

> "Its non-pecuniary awards serve to give recognition to the fact that moral damage occurred as a result of a breach of a fundamental human right and reflect in the broadest of terms the severity of the damage; they are not, nor should they be, intended to give financial comfort or sympathetic enrichment at the expense of the Contracting Party concerned."

9. The ECtHR has itself stated that "*it is not its role under Article 41 to function akin to a domestic tort mechanism court in apportioning fault and compensatory damages between civil parties. Its guiding principle is equity, which above all involves flexibility and an objective consideration of what is just, fair and reasonable in all the circumstances of the case.*"[17]

---

[17] *Al-Jedda v United Kingdom* (2011) 53 E.H.R.R. 789 at [114].

What that means when calculating the non-pecuniary award is not entirely clear.

10. The ECtHR has confirmed that the principle underlying the award of damages is *restitutio in integrum* (restoration to original condition),[18] which many English and Welsh lawyers will recognise as an underlying principle in calculating domestic tort damages. The practical reality is that the vindication of rights and compensatory damages is not mutually exclusive and should not be approached as such.

11. Asking whether there is a material impact on valuation, by viewing award of damages amounts to vindication of the right or to compensation of the loss, tends to distract from the other discernible principles on non-pecuniary damages.[19]

12. Lord Bingham suggested that the four discernible preconditions to an award of damages under section 8 HRA were:

    a. "*a finding of unlawfulness or prospective unlawfulness should be made based on breach or prospective breach by a public authority of a Convention right*";

    b. "*that the court should have power to award damages, or order the payment of compensation, in civil proceedings*";

    c. "*that the court should be satisfied, taking account of all the circumstances of the particular case, that an award of damages is necessary to afford just satisfaction to the person in whose favour it is made*";

---

18 *Kingsley v United Kingdom* (2002) 35 E.H.R.R. 10 at [40]; *R (Wilkinson) v Inland Revenue Commissioners* [2005] UKHL 30 at [26].

19 Leaving aside the debate about whether there are discernible principles that appears frequently elsewhere.

d. "*that the court should consider an award of damages to be just and appropriate*". But, the reason to separate the third and fourth precondition is unclear given the observation that if a court is satisfied that it is necessary to award non-pecuniary damages, "*it is hard to see how the court could consider it other than just and appropriate to do so.*"[20]

13. Conceptually, it is understandable that if a statement that a person's rights have been violated acknowledges the breach, no more is required; it is comparable with the acceptance of an apology over a financial sum. But, the breadth of rights protected and circumstances where rights may be violated makes the necessity test (third precondition) nebulous to consider a precondition.

14. The ECtHR's Practice Direction on Just Satisfaction[21] lists the factors the ECtHR takes into account when considering non-pecuniary damages (though some of these factors may be more comfortably considered by reference to the measure of damages rather than whether an award should be made at all):

    a. The ECtHR's starting point is its own practice in respect of similar violations.

    b. The nature and gravity of the violation.

    c. The duration and effect of the violation.

    d. Whether there have been several violations of the protected rights.

---

20 *R (Greenfield) v Secretary of State for the Home Department* [2005] UKHL 14 at [6].

21 See its applicability in *R (on the application of E) v Islington LBC* [2017] EWHC 1440 (Admin) at [147].

e. Whether other awards had been made.

f. Other measures taken that could be regarded as constituting an appropriate means of redress.

g. Any other context or case-specific circumstances, including the individual's contribution to the situation complained of.

15. The questions practitioners ought to ask themselves when considering whether damages are likely to be awarded are:

a. Has/have the violation(s) ended by the date the claim was issued?

b. Generally, in respect of the right violated (or allegedly so), have courts and/or the ECtHR awarded non-pecuniary damages for the violations or treated a finding/declaration as just satisfaction?

c. Has there been more than one act that has given rise to multiple violations of several rights in a single course of events?

d. Has the violation caused any material harm: physical or mental?

e. Is there a parallel claim, made in domestic law, for which the claimant should/will recover monetary damages?

f. Would the claimant's conduct render it just and appropriate to not make an award at all?[22]

---

22 This question comes up again in respect of the calculation of damages below.

Has the violation ended?

16. The reasons underpinning the creation of the Convention give primacy to securing the end of the violation, which is reflected in the structure of section 8 HRA.

17. In *Alseran v Ministry of Defence* [2017] EWHC 3289 (QB), Leggatt J, as he then was, observed that Lord Woolf CJ's comments in *Anufrijeva*, that damages had a less prominent role in the HRA claims, were concerned with cases where the breaches are continuing, but observed:

> "There are other cases, however, where the claimant is not seeking an essentially public law remedy of this kind and which fall into the category described by Laws LJ as 'cases where the violation of the Convention right has an outcome for the claimant which constitutes or is akin to a private wrong'.... In these cases, where the violation alleged is not continuing but purely historic, the concern is self-evidently not to bring the infringement of the claimant's human rights to an end as the infringement has already ended. In these cases the only remedy which the court can provide is an award of damages to compensate the claimant for the injury caused by the infringement. The question of compensation is therefore of primary, if not sole, importance. To decline to award damages, or to make an award which affords only partial reparation, would be to deny the claimant an effective remedy, contrary to principle and to the UK's obligation under article 13 of the Convention to afford an effective remedy to everyone whose Convention rights are violated."[23]

18. The approach potentially contradicts the view that the primacy of a finding of a violation/declaratory should not be forgotten nor

---

[23] At [933].

underestimated,[24] as the public vindication of the wrong suffered in a binding judgment is a powerful form of redress in itself.[25]

19. The relevance of whether the violation is continuing will depend on the particular right; for instance, damages have been awarded where there was a continuing violation of an absolute right and the continuation increased the likelihood of damages being awarded due to the duration of the breach.[26] By contrast, the fact that the public authority had taken steps to improve the process or procedures after the violation was immaterial to whether damages ought to be awarded,[27] but a failure to take any steps is likely to be relevant to gravity of the violation and may persuade the court to award non-pecuniary damages.

Articles of a kind

20. The starting point, for practitioners when assessing the likelihood and value of a non-pecuniary award, is to look at whether damages are generally awarded for a violation of a particular right. Each chapter below confirms the general approach in respect of that article.

21. The starting points, in respect of most violations, ought not to come as a surprise: for instance, where the violation involves physical or mental harm as a condition precedent (such as torture under Article 3), monetary awards are highly likely. Mere distress will not

---

24 *D and V v Commissioner of Police of the Metropolis* [2014] EWHC 2493 (QB) at [18].

25 *Varnava and others v Turkey* (Application nos. 16064/90 and others, 18 September 2009) at [224].

26 *Varnava and others v Turkey* (Application nos. 16064/90 and others, 18 September 2009) at [224].

27 *R (on the application of E) v Islington LBC* [2017] EWHC 1440 (Admin) at [152].

necessarily warrant an award of damages, the impact must be "*of such intensity*" to justify a non-pecuniary award.[28]

Several Violations

22. Where there have been several rights violations, the likelihood of damages being awarded appears to increase,[29] reflecting the seriousness of the damage.[30]

23. The relevance of several violations is not material where findings arise from a single act or omission. Its relevance arises from whether, over a course of events, there had been repeated separate actions/omissions (as opposed to a single decision maintained over a period of time) that led to a finding of a violation of a right[31] or several violations of different rights over the course of events.[32]

24. Practitioners ought to still consider whether monetary awards are generally made in respect of each of the rights allegedly violated, separately. If monetary damages are usually awarded in respect of one of the claimed violations, it is more likely than not the claim overall will result in the award of damages.

---

28 *Silver v United Kingdom* (1991) 13 E.H.R.R. 582 at [10].

29 See, by way of example, when awards are made in Article 6 cases at Chapter 6.

30 *Varnava and others v Turkey* (Application nos. 16064/90 and others, 18 September 2009) at [224].

31 See for example, *D and V v Commissioner of Police of the Metropolis* [2014] EWHC 436 (QB).

32 See for example, *GD and BD (by their Children's Guardian), MD and FD v Wakefield Metropolitan District Council and another* [2016] EWHC 3312 (Fam).

The existence of harm

25. The ECtHR's Practice Direction on Just Satisfaction explains that:

> "The purpose of the Court's award under Article 41 of the Convention in respect of damage is to compensate the applicant for the actual harmful consequences of a violation. No award can therefore be made for damage caused by events or situations that have not been found to constitute a violation of the Convention...."[33]

26. The burden of proving the existence of harm is on the individual, unless it finds that damage would have been a likely consequence of the breach,[34] which appears to be the reason that the ECtHR has inferred harm justifying non-pecuniary awards without the strict requirement for evidence of causation and/or injury.[35] The ECtHR considers whether the average person in the situation of the individual would have suffered harm, when inferring harm.[36] The ECtHR's approach to inferring harm feeds into the starting point in respect of a particular right (above at paragraph 20); if physical or mental harm/suffering is a pre-requisite to establishing a violation of

---

[33] At paragraph 2.

[34] *R (KB) v Mental Health Appeal Tribunal* [2003] EWHC 193 (Admin) at [24].

[35] *Van der Leer v The Netherlands* (1990) 12 E.H.R.R. 567 at [42].

[36] *Abdulaziz, Cabales and Balkandali v. the United Kingdom* (1985) 7 E.H.R.R. 471 at [96]; Altwicker-Hamori, Szilvia and Altwicker, Tilmann and Peters, Anne, *Measuring Violations of Human Rights: An Empirical Analysis of Awards in Respect of Non-Pecuniary Damage Under the European Convention on Human Rights* (July 16, 2015). Zeitschrift für ausländisches öffentliches Recht und Völkerrecht (ZaöRV)/Heidelberg Journal of International Law (HJIL) 76 (2016), 1-51, Available at SSRN: https://ssrn.com/abstract=2631404 or http://dx.doi.org/10.2139/ssrn.2631404.

the right, an inference of harm is more likely (though not inevitable).[37]

Parallel claim in domestic law

27. Section 8(3)(a) HRA specifically obliges the court to take into account any other remedy in relation to the act in question. Reference to "the act in question" as opposed to the violation instructs the courts to take into account damages for the conduct and outcome, as opposed to the legal rights/breaches. Accordingly, where a claimant has a claim in domestic law for the conduct and outcome, and is awarded damages for the same, such awards will be relevant to whether an award under the HRA should be made at all (as well as the value of a HRA award).

28. In *ZH (A protected party by GH, his litigation friend) v Commissioner of Police for the Metropolis* [2012] EWHC 604 (QB) at [158], the court concluded that the remedies obtained in the claims made under domestic law afforded just satisfaction making it inappropriate to make any award for damages under the HRA.

29. However, in *D and V v Commissioner of Police of the Metropolis* [2014] EWHC 2493 (QB), Green J stated that the extent to which parallel outcomes influence whether, and what, award for non-pecuniary damages should be made "*will necessarily vary from case to case and in a variety of different ways.*"[38]

30. It follows that if there is a parallel claim made under domestic law, which is successful, and damages for that claim would wholly compensate for the losses experienced by the claimant for the

37 See the discussion in *D and V v Commissioner of Police of the Metropolis* [2014] EWHC 2493 (QB), in particular the delineation of causes at [112].

38 At [55].

outcome of the conduct suffered, it serves little purpose to make a separate award for a HRA violation.

Claimant's conduct

31. The individual's conduct may be taken into account both at the stage of considering whether to make an award and the value of any monetary award.

32. In *McCann v United Kingdom* (1995) 21 E.H.R.R. 97, the ECtHR noted that the men killed by military forces in Gibraltar, who thereby thwarted a bomb plot and protected the public. The ECtHR concluded that it was not appropriate to make a monetary award because the three men killed had been terrorist suspects.

Calculation Principles

The award itself

33. The overarching principles to note, against which it is sensible to cross-check the final calculation, are:

    a. The awards of damages are modest[39] (though the reasons for modest awards in particular cases must be checked against the awards requested from the ECtHR).[40]

    b. Comparable domestic cases (and scales of damages), where the violation of the Convention right has an outcome similar

---

39 *Dobson v Thames Water Utilities Ltd* [2009] EWCA Civ 28 at [46]; *R (Greenfield) v Secretary of State for the Home Department* [2005] UKHL 14 at [17]; *R (Sturnham) v Parole Board* [2013] UKSC 23 at [13].

40 *D and V v Commissioner of Police of the Metropolis* [2014] EWHC 2493 (QB) at [68(2)]

to a private law wrong, are relevant but are not decisive of the relevant award.[41]

c. An award of damages at common law or pursuant to some other compensatory regime (such as ombudsman awards) may be taken into account, but are not decisive of whether a non-pecuniary award under the HRA should be made and the value of such award.[42]

34. Various approaches have been adopted by the courts on how to assess damages in cases concerning the violations of different rights. Assimilating the approaches, the questions for practitioners to ask themselves when assessing the likely value – applicable in respect of all violations – appears to be:

a. Was the alleged violation of a procedural guarantee or a substantive right?[43]

b. Did the individual suffer physical or mental diagnosable injury? If there is no expert evidence of loss, does the condition precedent of the violation involve physical or

---

41 *Z v United Kingdom* (2002) 34 E.H.R.R. 97 at [120] and [131]; *Alseran v Ministry of Defence* [2017] EWHC 3289 (QB) at [930, 931, 939 – 942] where Leggatt J, as he then was, considered it was not only relevant to take into account domestic scales of compensation but important to do so. Confirming that domestic scales of compensation are more than simply relevant has not yet been confirmed by the Supreme Court or ECtHR.

42 *Dobson v Thames Water Utilities Ltd* [2009] EWCA Civ 28 at [52]; *D and V v Commissioner of Police of the Metropolis* [2014] EWHC 2493 (QB) at [14].

43 *R (Greenfield) v Secretary of State for the Home Department* [2005] UKHL 14 at [7], though in respect of Article 3 violations the impact of the distinction between procedural and substantive obligations on damages is limited (*D and V v Commissioner of Police of the Metropolis* [2014] EWHC 2493 (QB) at [68(4)]).

mental harm? Expert evidence may result in a larger award,[44] though whether the expert evidence proves more than the reasonably anticipated suffering may be relevant to the question of costs later.

c. If so, what are those injuries (or losses if the harm does not involve personal injury, such as a deprivation of liberty)?[45]

d. Was the loss/harm caused by the violation:

    i. If "but for" causation can be proved, then the answer on causation is clearly established.

    ii. If the violation is one of the material causes of the loss, then causation is likely to be established.

    iii. In cases concerning the operational duties under Articles 2, 3 and/or 4, causation is established for the harm where the reasonable steps had a substantial chance of averting the outcome (reflecting the fourth stage of *Osman* where the steps "might have been expected to avoid that risk"[46]).

e. If the counterfactual is purely speculative, causation is unlikely to be established.[47]

---

44 *D and V v Commissioner of Police of the Metropolis* [2014] EWHC 2493 (QB) at [68(1)].

45 *Alseran v Ministry of Defence* [2017] EWHC 3289 (QB) at [937].

46 *Osman v United Kingdom* (2000) 29 E.H.R.R. 245 at [116].

47 *Re Mahmud's Application for Judicial Review* [2021] NIQB 37 at [42] – [44], [55].

f. Is there a comparable private law right with the Convention right (even if the claimant had not made a claim based on domestic law)?[48]

   i. If so, what is the domestic approach to damages? What sum would be awarded for those injuries/losses if applying domestic damages principles?[49]

   ii. If not, what is the previous practice of the awards in respect of the specific rights in the UK, or in ECtHR? Or indeed, does the answer take you back to the questions on whether non-pecuniary damages ought to be awarded at all?[50]

g. Are there any reasons to depart from or adjust the sum calculated, for example:

   i. Could the individual be considered to be culpable, to have contributed to or to have acted in such a way as to reduce the potential compensation payable?[51]

---

48 *R (on the application of E) v Islington LBC* [2017] EWHC 1440 (Admin) suggested that the domestic court should look first at the Strasbourg case law before then looking at the potential award under domestic law, and then undertake a comparison between the two values (at [147(2)]). By contrast, the court in *Alseran v Ministry of Defence* [2017] EWHC 3289 (QB) at [938] suggests that (after the injury/loss is identified) assess the compensation by reference to domestic law principles.

49 *Alseran v Ministry of Defence* [2017] EWHC 3289 (QB) at [938].

50 *R (on the application of SXC) v Secretary of State for Work and Pensions* [2019] EWHC 2774 (Admin) at [13].

51 *Johnson v United Kingdom* (1999) 27 E.H.R.R. 296 at [77].

ii. Has the individual received compensation through other mechanism for the outcome underpinning the violation?

iii. What other redress has been granted?

h. At the end of the calculation, is the calculated value of the possible award significantly more or less generous than the amount the ECtHR would be expected to award?

Aggravation and mitigation

35. Lord Woolf CJ in *Anufrijeva v London Borough of Southwark and others* [2003] EWCA Civ 1406 expressly stated that *"exemplary damages are not awarded"* in HRA claims.[52]

36. The continuing practice of the ECtHR is to reject claims for aggravated and/or punitive damages.[53] The ECtHR's Practice Direction on Just Satisfaction, updated in 2022, maintains that position explaining that non-pecuniary awards are:

> "not intended to punish the Contracting Party responsible. The Court has therefore considered it inappropriate to accept claims for damages with labels such as "punitive", "aggravated" or "exemplary"; nor does the Court make symbolic awards."

Adjustment, inflation, and interest

37. In Green J's decision on remedy in *D and V v Commissioner of Police of the Metropolis* [2014] EWHC 2493 (QB) at [34-35], he noted:

> "34. It seems to me that awards made by the Strasbourg court in relation to applicants resident in countries with a

52 At [55(e)].

53 *Greens and M.T. v. the United Kingdom* (2011) 53 E.H.R.R. 21 at [97].

> different standard of living than the UK may still be relevant provided one applies to the quantum of the award an appropriate adjustment factor to take account of differences in the cost of living. …
>
> 35. A reflection of the need for temporal adjustment factors is also found in the observation of Lord Reed JSC in the Sturnham case [2013] 2 AC 254, para 74 that although the court does not make precise adjustments to reflect inflation it is necessary to bear in mind that some of the awards were made many years ago. An express articulation of the fact that the Strasbourg court takes inflation into account is the interesting dissent of Judge Garlicki in the Grand Chamber judgment in Vistiņš v Latvia[54]…"

38. To limit the extent of adjustments required for awards referenced in this book that concerning other countries, the options have focussed on cases of a similar GDP as the UK, but practitioners will need to consider the adjustment for inflation and set the outcome of the calculation against more recent non-pecuniary awards for violations of the particular right (and where available for similar circumstances). Consequently, each report includes the date of judgment to assist in calculating inflation.

39. The practice of the ECtHR is to award default interest at the lending rate of the European Central Bank plus three percentage points. Otherwise, interest on top of the award does not feature in the ECtHR caselaw; the award itself wholly reflects just satisfaction.

---

[54] (2014) 58 E.H.R.R. 107 and 59 E.H.R.R. 817, at [3], where Judge Garlicki stated that the calculation of the award made by the majority "has been almost doubled due to the inflation rate. While this is the usual method of calculation, its application in the present case has led to over-generous effects."

CHAPTER THREE

ARTICLES 2 AND 3

<u>*Article 2*</u>

1. Everyone's right to life shall be protected by law. No one shall be deprived of his life intentionally save in the execution of a sentence of a court following his conviction of a crime for which this penalty is provided by law.

2. Deprivation of life shall not be regarded as inflicted in contravention of this Article when it results from the use of force which is no more than absolutely necessary:

(a) in defence of any person from unlawful violence;

(b) in order to effect a lawful arrest or to prevent the escape of a person lawfully detained;

(c) in action lawfully taken for the purpose of quelling a riot or insurrection.

<u>*Article 3*</u>

No one shall be subjected to torture or to inhuman or degrading treatment or punishment.

Introduction and principles

1. The case law concerning violations of Articles 2 and 3 can be analogous.[55] Principles applicable to the award of non-pecuniary damages for violations of Articles 2 and 3 share common features. Both are absolute rights, from which no derogation may be permitted, even during a state of emergency, and rank as the most fundamental provisions of the convention. Accordingly, the right to an effective remedy, protected by Article 13, often demands the availability of monetary awards for violations of those rights (*Keenan v United Kingdom* (2001) 33 E.H.R.R. 38). This chapter is organised by reference to categories of case, rather than by right alone.

2. In Article 2 and Article 3 cases, just satisfaction often requires that a non-pecuniary award will be made for pain, stress, anxiety, and frustration for a violation of Article 2 or 3, regardless of the type of violation.[56] The value of the award will depend on the level of the authority's culpability.

3. Examples of where no award for damages were made by the ECtHR arise where the applicant has not sought such an award (*McCaughey v United Kingdom* (2014) 58 E.H.R.R. 13) or when the ECtHR has regard to the conduct of the applicant (*McCann v United Kingdom* (1996) 21 E.H.R.R. 97 and, arguably, *Vinter v United Kingdom* (2016) 63 E.H.R.R. 1) though the court did not explicitly suggest that the conduct/profile of the applicant impacted the decision not to award non-pecuniary damages.

---

55 *D and V v Commissioner of Police of the Metropolis* [2014] EWHC 2493 (QB) at [66].

56 *D and V v Commissioner of Police of the Metropolis* [2014] EWHC 2493 (QB) at [68(4)].

4. In *Savage v South Essex Partnership NHS Foundation Trust* [2010] EWHC 865 (QB) at [97],[57] the court observed that the range of awards for violations of Article 2 made by the ECtHR were between €5,000 and €60,000 (£4,372 and £52,466 at 28 April 2010).[58]

5. As the claimant is often a family member in Article 2 cases, Lord Dyson considered the relevant factors in considering non-pecuniary awards in Article 2 cases included:

> "... the closeness of the family link between the victim and the deceased, the nature of the breach and the seriousness of the non-pecuniary damage that the victim has suffered. Factors which will tend to place the amount of the award towards the upper end of the range are the existence of a particularly close family tie between the victim and the deceased; the fact that the breach is especially egregious; and the fact that the circumstances of the death and the authority's response to it have been particularly distressing to the victims. Conversely, factors which will tend to place the award towards the lower end of the range are the weakness of the family ties, the fact that the breach is towards the lower end of the scale of gravity and the fact that the circumstances of the death have not caused the utmost distress to the victims."[59]

6. In *D and V v Commissioner of Police of the Metropolis* [2014] EWHC 2493 (QB), Green J observed that the range of awards for psychological/mental or other harm for similar violations of Articles

---

57 Which followed the appeals up to the House of Lords – [2008] UKHL 74.

58 Exchange rate €1.1436 to £1.

59 *Rabone and another v Pennine Care NHS Trust (Inquest and others intervening)* [2012] UKSC 2 at [85].

2 and 3, having taken into account adjustment factors for cost of living and inflation by 23 July 2014, were:

a. €1,000 to €8,000 (£804 to £6,433), where the ECtHR wished to make a nominal or low award;

b. €8,000 to €20,000 (£6,433 to £16,082), for routine violations with no serious long term mental health issues and no unusual aggravating features;

c. €20,000 to €100,000+ (£16,082 to £80,412+) for cases where there were features such as medical evidence of material psychological harm; harm amounting to a recognised medical condition; where the victim had also suffered physical harm or a crime caused in part by the state; long term systemic/endemic failings by the state; and/or morally reprehensible conduct by the state.[60]

7. Green J stated the main factors he took into account were (at [118]):

a. The nature of the harm suffered and treatment costs;

b. The duration of the breach;

c. The nature of the failings;

d. Whether the failings were operational and/or systemic;

e. The overall context to the violations;

f. Whether there was bad faith on the part of the defendant;

g. Whether there is any other reason why an enhanced award should be made; where the award sits on the range of awards made by Strasbourg and in similar domestic cases;

---

60 Exchange rate €1.2436 to £1.

h. Other payments;

i. Totality and modesty.

8. In cases concerning Article 3 violations, in the first instance, relief will be achieved by the cessation of treatment amounting to a violation. Compensation will not be a sufficient remedy in response to ongoing treatment.

Detention

Custody

England and Wales

VG v First-tier Tribunal and the Criminal Injuries Compensation Authority [2017] UKUT 0049 (AAC), 3 February 2017

Summary: the case concerned the repayment of a criminal injuries compensation award for the death of VG's son, K, who was stabbed by Mr A, who had a diagnosis of paranoid schizophrenia and was a resident of a care home for those with mental health needs. Knives had been confiscated from Mr A on several occasions in the years prior to K's death. In the week prior to Mr A killing K, Mr A had been non-compliant with his medication. The claim was settled. The judgment of the Upper Tribunal notes that counsel valued the damages for a breach of the systemic duty alone. The Upper Tribunal noted that the settlement was premised on the basis of the "settlement of the whole of the claim".

Key Points:

- Systems Duty.
- Article 2.
- Settlement.
- Third party killing.
- Mental health detainee.

Award: £10,000.

Douglas v Ministry of Justice and Care UK [2018] Inquest LR 71, 8 January 2018

Summary: This was a costs case following settlement of a claim for damages arising from the death of Imran Douglas, D, who had hung himself in his cell in prison, a month after he received a life sentence, with a tariff of 18 years, for murder. The jury found that D's death had been contributed to by a lack of transition planning on his transfer to prison, arising out of a failure to draft and prepare a transition plan (despite there being an instruction from the Head of Young People that one should be prepared), mental health assessments by the healthcare provider were perfunctory, and no one had considered opening an ACCT (Assessment, Care in Custody, and Teamwork) care planning case to support D. The National Offender Management Service, under the remit of the Ministry of Justice, admitted liability for claims in negligence and breaches of the HRA.

Key Points:

- Operational Duty.
- Article 2.
- Settlement.
- Suicide.
- Joint defendants.
- Damages for common law claim.

Award: £13,500.

ECtHR

Keenan v United Kingdom (2001) 33 E.H.R.R. 38, 3 April 2001

Summary: MK was serving a prison sentence for assault of his girlfriend. He had established diagnoses of paranoid schizophrenia and borderline personality disorder. MK had resided in the healthcare centre and in the ordinary prison location. Prior to his death, when on ordinary location, MK's cellmate reported that MK had fashioned a noose from a bed sheet, which prompted MK's return to the healthcare centre. Nine days prior to his anticipated released date, MK faced an adjudication for the assault of two officers and was sentenced to 28 additional days in prison, with 7 days loss of association and exclusion from work in segregation. The next day, MK hung himself from the bars of his cell, using a bedsheet ligature. The ECtHR found no violation of Article 2 but concluded that there had been a violation of Article 3. There was an inadequate concern by prison doctors to ensure full and detailed records, a lack of effective monitoring, lack of informed psychiatric input, and the imposition of a further 28 days' imprisonment, threatened his physical and moral resistance such that it constituted inhuman and degrading treatment.

Key Points:

- Operational Duty.
- Article 3.
- No Article 2 violation.
- Suicide.

Award: £7,000 to MK's estate. A separate award of £3,000 was made to the applicant for her distress from the circumstances of MK's detention and inability to pursue an effective avenue of redress.

Healthcare

Savage v South Essex Partnership NHS Foundation Trust [2010] EWHC 865 (QB), 28 April 2010

Summary: Ms Savage, "CS", who had a diagnosis of paranoid schizophrenia, was detained pursuant to section 3 of the Mental Health Act 1983 for treatment. She had several admissions under the MHA. The risk assessments stated CS was a low risk of suicide and/or self-harm but a high risk of absconding. When she did so, CS walked to a train station and jumped in front of a train. The court found that the Trust knew or ought to have known that CS was a suicide risk, she had made numerous attempts to abscond, there were no proper risk assessments or consideration of the level of observations CS should have been subject to reduce her risk of absconding, and there was no reasonable basis to conclude CS's presentation was improving. CS's daughter stated that the primary purpose of the claim was not for financial award, though it was submitted on her behalf that £30,000 would be appropriate in this case.

Key Points:

- Operational duty.
- Article 2.
- Suicide.

Award: £10,000.

Rabone and another v Pennine Care NHS Trust [2012] UKSC 2, 8 February 2012

Summary: M was a voluntary psychiatric patient undergoing treatment at a psychiatric unit for a depressive disorder. She had been admitted following a suicide attempt. M had been assessed as a moderate to high risk of further suicide attempt. The clinician who had assessed her risk granted M two days' home leave, including overnight, despite concerns raised about M's condition by M's parents. During her home leave, M went to the park and hanged herself from a tree. The trust had admitted liability in negligence but disputed a breach of Article 2. Damages in negligence had been paid in the sum of £7,500 on behalf of M's estate. M's risk of suicide was real and immediate when M was allowed home. The trust's admission of liability for negligence indicated that the decision to allow M home was a decision that no reasonable psychiatric practitioner would have made.

Key Points:

- Operational Duty.
- Article 2.

- Suicide.
- Separate damages for common law claim.

Award: £5,000 for each claimant, which was left undisturbed by the Supreme Court.

Briley v Leicestershire Partnership NHS Trust, University Hospitals Leicester NHS Trust [2023] EWHC 1470 (SCCO), 9 June 2023

Summary: A costs case arising from a settlement following an inquest. Amanda Briley, AB, ligatured herself and died from having suffered an un-survivable hypoxic brain injury in a hospital unit considered by all professionals to be wholly unsuitable for her needs. AB had suffered from self-harming, including suicidal, behaviours and mental health difficulties since she was 12 years old. She had a diagnosis of Asperger's Syndrome and emotional unstable personality disorder. AB had had very limited leave. AB was allowed to return home for Christmas. It was anticipated that AB's return to the unit from home leave could leave to her experiencing extreme confusion and distress. The plan was for the frequency of observations of AB on the ward to reduce in the lead up to her home leave, and to increase following her return from leave. When AB returned from home leave, the level of observations was not increased to constant supervision in line with the plan.

Key Points:

- Article 2.
- Operational Duty.
- Settlement.
- Suicide.
- Damages for common law claim.

Award: £65,000. A global figure to reflect breaches of AB, her brother's and her parents' Convention rights, as well as non HRA claims. Apportioning by percentage of the initial valuation of the claim suggests the valuation for breaches of Article 2 varied between 14% and 18% of the damages sought, as such, the awards accepted were £9,100 for AB and her brother's rights, and £11,700 for her parents.

Security

Alseran and others v Ministry of Defence [2017] EWHC 3298 (QB), 14 December 2017

Summary: Various claims by Iraqi civilians for unlawful imprisonment and ill-treatment during the United Kingdom's participation in the military action in Iraq from 2003 to 2009. The Article 3 claims related to allegations of assault by the British military:

- Alseran: soldiers ran over their backs;
- MRE: hooded with a sandbag during transportation and sustained an eye injury from a small sharp object inside the sandbag; struck on the head and kicked in the knee.
- KSU: hooded with a sandbag during transportation;
- Al-Waheed: assault on the upper back and arms and punched in the face; harsh interrogation; sleep deprivation for a day and a half; sight and hearing deprivation for 12 hours following arrest and whenever out of his cell for a period of 13 days.

Key Points:

- Article 3.
- Negative Duty.
- Military intervention.
- Separate awards for Article 5 breaches (see Chapter 5).

Awards:

- Alseran: £10,000.

- MRE: £10,000 for hooding; £1,000 for eye injury; £15,000 for head injury; £1,400 for medical treatment.
- KSU: £10,000 for hooding.
- Al-Waheed: £15,000 for beating after arrest; £15,000 for harsh interrogation; sleep deprivation and sensory deprivation.

Criminal Justice

Jordan v Police Service of Northern Ireland [2019] NICA 61, 15 November 2019

Summary: J was shot and killed by a member of the Royal Ulster Constabulary in 1992. An inquest followed. The case went to the ECtHR. The ECtHR had awarded £10,000 for a breach of Article 2 arising from a failure to carry out a prompt and effective investigation. The inquest conclusion (then verdict) was quashed, and the inquest remitted. These proceedings alleged breaches of the Article 2 procedural duty due to delays in the inquest. The PSNI had failed to disclose relevant information and delayed in commencing the process of a risk assessment relating to the anonymity of witnesses. The period of unlawful delay for which PSNI was responsible was between March 2007 and May 2008.

Key Points:

- Article 2.
- Procedural Duty.
- Police.
- Delays to inquest.

Award: £5,000 considering the award already made by the ECtHR and the short period of delay for which PSNI was culpable.

Goodenough v Chief Constable of Thames Valley [2020] EWHC 1428 (QB),[61] 26 March 2020

Summary: In 2003, Robin Goodenough, G, was driving his sister's car under the influence of butane (liquid petroleum gas) with his sister as a passenger. He was pursued by the police. When the vehicles stopped, G refused to exit the car and prevented officers from opening the car doors. Multiple attempts were made by the police to physically extract G from the vehicle. When G was pulled from the vehicle, G's face hit the road. He sustained a fracture to his alveolar ridge (the raised thickened border of the jaw that contains the sockets of the teeth). The cause of death was atrial fibrillation caused by the stress of events. The Article 2 claim was successful because the investigation was seriously operationally inadequate; the officers had had the opportunity to discuss the events before giving their statements and were debriefed collectively. Although there was no evidence of collusion, there was a risk of innocent contamination in the officers' accounts. The shortcomings of the investigation added to the distress and anxiety suffered by the claimants.

Key Points:

- Article 2.
- Investigative Duty.
- Police.
- Appearance of collusion.
- Delays to trial.

Award: £5,000 for each claimant.

---

[61] Appeal concerned the claim in negligence that had been dismissed – [2021] EWCA Civ 1422.

OOO, OOA, MTK, RTF v Commissioner of Police for the Metropolis [2011] EWHC 1246 (QB), 20 May 2011

Summary: The claimants alleged that the police infringed their Article 3 and 4 rights by failing to investigate their being trafficked from Nigeria and forced into modern slavery. They were required to work without pay for long hours (between 17 and 22 hours a day), for households in and around London and were subjected to physical and emotional abuse by the householders. The abuse included beatings with hands, shoes, rulers, ladles, sticks and other objects. The court concluded that there was a failure to investigate allegations from other complainants, including taking their detailed statements, which would have identified the claimants as victims of trafficking and modern slavery thereby enabling the police to take steps to intervene to protect them. Further, following the claimants' complaints, there was no investigation by the police. An undertaking to investigate was promised 18 months after the initial complaint by the claimants. The award recognised the frustration and anxiety experienced for over a period of 12 to 15 months.

Key Points:

- Article 3.
- Investigative Duty.
- Third party conduct.
- Parallel Article 4 claim.

Award: £5,000 per claimant in respect of both Article 3 and 4.

C v Chief Constable of Northern Ireland [2020] NIQB 3, 13 January 2020

Summary: C complained that the failure to conduct a proper investigation into her allegation of rape breached Articles 3 and 8, which caused extreme upset, distress, and psychiatric injury including self-harming, depression, psychotic symptoms, and an eating disorder. C had a diagnosis of Asperger's syndrome. There was no prosecution of the alleged assailant. C received a compensation payment of £22,500 under the Criminal Injuries Compensation Scheme. The court identified that the operational failures were:

- Failures and/or delays to obtain statements – No enquiries made of named witnesses. No attempts to seek a social worker to speak with an important witness, who also suffered from Asperger's Syndrome.

- Failures to follow investigative leads – No house-to-house enquiries were undertaken to establish the location of the assault. No CCTV was viewed or seized. No attempt was made to follow up C's assertion that she had left personal items at the scene of the assault.

- Failures and/or delays to securing and processing evidence: Failures to make a meaningful attempt to access C's diary or her mobile. Failure to submit material for forensic science analysis.

- Failures to review the strategy when it was apparent that an Achieving Best Evidence interview was to be delayed and a failure by supervising officers to change the strategy.

- The absence of training on the policy documentation, on Child Abuse and Rape Enquiry units and the arrangements for close liaison between Police Service of Northern Ireland and Social Services, was a systemic failing. Officers accepted disciplinary sanctions and accepted they failed to conduct a thorough investigation. The former Chief Constable had offered an unreserved apology.

Key Points:

- Article 3.
- Investigative Duty.
  Third party conduct.
- No separate Article 8 finding.

Award: £15,000.

R (AXO) v First-tier Tribunal and the Criminal Injuries Compensation Authority [2024] EWCA Civ 226, 11 March 2024[62]

Summary: the case concerned the repayment of a criminal injuries compensation award for the death of AXO's mother. AXO's mother was killed by her former partner. After Criminal Injuries Compensation Authority ("**CICA**") awarded £25,500 to AXO for bereavement and loss of parental services, a human rights claim was lodged on AXO's behalf against the police, local authority and Secretary of State for Justice alleging breaches of Articles 2, 3, 8 and 14, as well as claims in tort. The claim was settled and subject to infant settlement approval by the High Court. Although the case itself was about repayments to CICA, the breakdown of settlement approved by the court assists with awards made under Articles 2 and 3 for breaches by the public authorities.

Key Points:

- Articles 2 and 3.
- Investigative Duty.
- Settlement.
- Third party killing.
- Damages for common law claim.

Award:

- £10,000 for a breach of Article 2, to reflect AXO's mother's loss of life and failure to protect that right.
- £5,000 for the breach of Article 3, for the failure to properly investigate the circumstances of the inhuman and degrading treatment AXO was subject to.

[62] The settlement was approved on 17 September 2019.

D and V v Commissioner of Police of the Metropolis [2014] EWHC 2493 (QB), 23 July 2014

Summary: D and V were victims of a convicted serial rapist, JW, who had given drugs and alcohol to passengers in his taxicab and sexually assaulted them. D and V had received compensation payments from CICA and had received payments from JW from their civil claim against him (£10,000 each from JW and £13,500 and £2,000 respectively from CICA). A breach of Article 3 arose from egregious and significant failures in the investigation, namely: failures to record relevant names, addresses and vehicle registration numbers from complainants; failure to interview a vital witness; failure to collect relevant and/or follow up CCTV evidence; failure to treat D's complaint seriously (on the basis she was intoxicated with drugs and/or alcohol) and the investigation was wrongly closed; failures to use intelligence sources; failures to conduct searches of JW's home; failures in the interview approach; failures to record incidents as a serious sexual offence. Had the failures not occurred, the court found D would not have experienced post-assault mental suffering and V would not have been raped at all. Awards were also made for future treatment. The decision on awards for non-pecuniary damages were left undisturbed by the Supreme Court ([2018] UKSC 11).

Key Points:

- Article 3.
- Investigative Duty.
- Systems Duty.
- Third party conduct.
- Compensation by others.

Award:

- D: £20,000.
- V: £17,000.

R (B) v Director of Public Prosecutions [2009] EWHC 106 (Admin), 27 January 2009

Summary: the claimant brought a claim for judicial review against the decision of the Crown Prosecution Service ("**CPS**") to discontinue a prosecution against a person, who the claimant alleged had wounded them with intent to cause grievous bodily harm. The CPS determined that the claimant would not be a reliable witness, because of their history of psychotic illness. No evidence was offered against the suspected assailant. The claimant alleged a violation of his Article 3 rights or, in the alternative, Article 8 and/ or 14 rights. The court held that the decision not to prosecute for this reason was irrational. The CPS's reasons caused him humiliation and amounted to a breach of his rights under Article 3. The damages were awarded to compensate him for the loss of opportunity of having a trial and for the way that he was made to feel that he was "beyond the effective protection of the law".

Key points:

- Article 3.
- Investigative Duty.
- Refusal to prosecute.

Award: £8,000.

Social Services

Z and others v United Kingdom (2002) 34 E.H.R.R. 3, 10 May 2001

Summary: the three applicants, A, B, C, and Z, were siblings subjected to abuse and neglect by their parents. Reports were made to the local authority from the school that A and B were craving for food (including taking food from the school bins), A was ill-kempt and dirty, Z and B were presenting as withdrawn and lacking vitality, and there were concerns the children's needs were not being met at home. The family home was noted to be filthy. There were several reports of the children having bruising to their face and body. The children were soiling themselves frequently, had poorly developed social skills, and difficulty sleeping. The children were accommodated by the local authority on a voluntary basis on several occasions. Eventually, the children's mother told the local authority that it must accommodate the children or she "would batter them". Care orders were applied for four and a half years after concerns were first noted by the local authority. During care proceedings, the expert evidence was that the children all showed evidence of psychological disturbance. The Grand Chamber did not expand on its reasons for finding a breach of Article 3, but the Commission (whose decision was considered by the Grand Chamber) concluded that the local authority failed to take reasonable steps to safeguard the children's welfare when initial steps did not result in an improvement in the home and family environment. The local authority had overlooked the signs that the children were suffering physical and psychological damage and delayed in convening a child protection case conference, decided not to place the children on the at risk register, did not assign a senior social worker to the family, and no steps were taken to obtain psychological assessments of the Z. Awards were also made for future medical expenses.

Key Points:

- Article 3.
- Operational Duty.
- Third party conduct.
- Expert evidence.

Award: £32,000 for each applicant.

E and other v United Kingdom (2003) 36 E.H.R.R. 31, 26 November 2002

Summary: the four applicants had suffered extensive sexual and physical abuse by their stepfather WH, when they were children. He was convicted of assaulting E and L and sentenced to two years' probation.

WH was not permitted to live at the family home, but social services records note suspicions that WH had returned to the family home. 10 years after WH's first conviction in respect of E and L, E, L and T reported a history of abuse by WH, and charges were brought against him. In a claim for compensation to CICA, the applicants reported the following abuse by WH and their suffering:

- E – 10 years of physical and sexual abuse. Daily physically abuse by WH; being forced to masturbate WH; digital penetration. The children were made to hit each other with chains and whips. E made several suicide attempts, developed a drinking problem, diagnosed with severe PTSD.

- H (the only male child) – physically abused. The children were made to hit each other with chains and whips. He had long term relationship problems; poor self-confidence; and personality difficulties.

- L – 10 years of physical and sexual abuse, and two further occasions when she was visiting her mother after she left home. WH touched her genitals and sexually touched her daily. When she was older, she was required to masturbate WH and perform oral sex on him, and eventually forced to have intercourse. The children were made to hit each other with chains and whips. She was diagnosed with severe post-traumatic stress disorder.

- T – 18 years of physical and sexual abuse. From the age of 9 she recalled WH sleeping in her bed naked; she was forced to touch and masturbate him two or three times a week; from age 14 she was forced to have sexual intercourse on one occasion and continued to be forced to masturbate him and perform oral sex.

The court concluded that the local authority ought to have been aware of the abuse given the records of E and L's presentation, WH's suspected residence in the family home, and WH's non-acceptance of the seriousness of the charges. Social services failed to take steps to discover the extent of the issues and thereby prevent further abuse taking place.

Key Points:

- Article 3.
- Operational Duty.
- Third party conduct.
- Compensation by others.

Award: €16,000 (£10,195) for E, H, and L and €32,000 (£20,390) to T for pecuniary and non-pecuniary damages, taking into account awards made by CICA and difficulties attributing damage caused by the failures of social services.[63]

Immigration

R (W) v Secretary of State for the Home Department [2020] EWHC 1299 (Admin), 21 May 2020

Summary: challenge to policy and practice of the Secretary of State for the Home Department ("**SSHD**") imposing the condition on the claimant's mother's visa to maintain and accommodate herself and any dependents without recourse to public funds ("**NRPF condition**"). It was alleged the NRPF condition contravened Article 3, as it would be imposed unless the individual provided evidence of destitution, thereby failing to ensure that imposing NRPF would not result in inhuman treatment. The regime for whether to impose the NRPF condition on the grant of leave to remain was unlawful, as the instructions did not oblige Home Office caseworkers to decide not to impose the NRPF condition, or oblige caseworkers to lift the NRPF condition, if the

63 Exchange rate €1.5694 to £1.

applicant would imminently suffer destitution and consequently gave rise to a real risk of unlawful decisions.

Key Points:

- Article 3.
- Systems Duty.
- Settlement following draft judgment.
- Destitution.
- Policy challenge.

Award: £3,000.

R (DMA, AHK, BK and ELN) v Secretary of State for the Home Department [2020] EWHC 3416 (Admin), 14 December 2020

Summary: the case concerned delays of between 45 days to nine months by the SSHD in providing asylum accommodation within a matter of days, following the decision that the individual was entitled to asylum accommodation.

Key Points:

- Article 3.
- Operational Duty.
- Destitution.
- Delay.

Award: £1,000 to each claimant.

ASY v Home Office [2024] EWCA Civ 373, 18 May 2024

Summary: Following the trial of a preliminary issue on whether a person subjected to the NRPF condition (referenced in *R (W) v Secretary of State for the Home Department* above) would have a right to damages for breach of their rights under Article 3, the first instance court concluded that (i) they did have a right to claim damages and (ii) such damages were quantified as £2,000 for each adult and £500 for each child, because of the differing levels of distress that would be experienced by the adult and the child. The court did not confirm that the awards were payable but indicated that the quantification of the award would be appropriate if the individual had suffered inhuman and/or degrading treatment as a result of the NRPF condition.

Key Points:

- Article 3.
- Systems Duty.
- Destitution.
- Policy challenge.

Award: £2,000 for each adult and £500 for each child (potentially).

CHAPTER FOUR

ARTICLE 4

1. No one shall be held in slavery or servitude.

2. No one shall be required to perform forced or compulsory labour.

3. For the purpose of this Article the term "forced or compulsory labour" shall not include:

(a) any work required to be done in the ordinary course of detention imposed according to the provisions of Article 5 of this Convention or during conditional release from such detention;

(b) any service of a military character or, in case of conscientious objectors in countries where they are recognised, service exacted instead of compulsory military service;

(c) any service exacted in case of an emergency or calamity threatening the life or well-being of the community;

(d) any work or service which forms part of normal civic obligations.

Introduction and principles

1. Article 4 enshrines the now universal acceptance that a person is more than a device for their output. Articles 4(1) and (2) are absolute rights from which no derogation is permissible. The restrictions on Article 4(3), forced or compulsory labour are subject to extremely limited circumstances.

2. One of the sad legal realisations of the 21st century has been that the right not to be enslaved or subjected to forced labour remains a continuing concern on modern society. An area where Article 4 emerges in the modern day is in the realm of human trafficking, though the event of human trafficking alone does not always engage Article 4.

3. It is fortunate to note that the Article 4 cases that have been dealt with in English and Welsh courts do not concern state-endorsed slavery, servitude, nor forced/compulsory labour. The focus of cases that have been litigated in the courts has been the positive obligations under Article 4 in dealing with non-state actors: to combat the violation of such rights by an effective system; to protect individuals from such violations where the authorities are aware there is a real and immediate risk of a person's rights being violated; and investigating potential violations of Article 4.

4. Three observations can be made about damages for Article 4 violations.

    a. Firstly, the challenges founded on failures to comply with positive obligations under Article 4, more so than in Article 2 and Article 3 cases, result in outcomes aimed at the cessation of a continuing failure to comply with the positive obligation.

    b. Secondly, as is understandable, often a violation of Article 4 will be closely related to a commensurate violation of Article 3, as seen in *OOO, OOA, MTK, RTF v Commissioner of Police for the Metropolis* [2011] EWHC 1246 (QB) in the previous chapter. A violation of Article 4 is not easily distinguished from a violation of Article 3; and the assessment of just satisfaction reflects this.

    c. Thirdly, compensation for violations of Article 4, especially concerning forced labour, may be addressed through the domestic employment laws, but, in that sphere, damages are awarded by reference to the applicable domestic regime rather than through the HRA (see for instance *A v Abu* [2017] EWHC 3098 (QB)), which makes the quantification of damages a challenge for Article 4 violations.

5. This chapter addresses the cases where no award for damages was made; where damages were ordered holistically including violation of other Articles of the ECHR; and cases concerning damages for Article 4 alone. There are more cases here where no awards for non-pecuniary damage were made and from the ECtHR than in other chapters, including cases concerning states in Europe, not just those with similar GDP to the United Kingdom, because of the limited number of cases concerning Article 4 violations.

No award

England and Wales

R (Atamewan) v Secretary of State for the Home Department [2013] EWHC 2727 (Admin), 6 September 2013

Summary: The case concerned the defendant's failure to initiate an effective investigation by the police in relation to historic allegations of trafficking. Atamewan was treated as an unpaid servant of her aunts in her country of origin. She then accompanied another adult to the UK to be a carer for that person's child without pay. She ran away and presented an asylum claim four years after her escape. The Article 4 violation was based on the failure of the defendant to notify the police to start an investigation. When Atamewan's solicitors notified the police, they took little action.

Key Points:

- Servitude.
- Trafficking.
- Domestic Service.

- Investigative Duty.

Award: None because the court could not identify any breach by the defendant (as distinct from any breach by the police) was causative of damages. A declaration was made.

R (TDT(Vietnam)) v Secretary of State for the Home Department [2018] EWCA Civ 1394, 19 June 2018

Summary: The Refugee Council concluded TDT was a child that had been trafficked to the UK. The defendant released TDT from detention without a move to safe accommodation. TDT disappeared. TDT's representatives started proceedings alleged the failure to take measures to prevent a real and immediate risk that he would be re-trafficked thereby breaching Article 4, although TDT could not be found.

Key Points:

- Trafficking.
- Re-trafficked.
- Criminal Enterprise.
- Operational Duty.

Award: None. A declaration was made. The absence of TDT meant that the declaration may be the foundation of a claim for damages later.

ECtHR

Siliadin v France (Application no. 73316/01), 26 October 2005

Summary: Siliadin moved to France with a visa from Togo to work for Mrs D, as an unpaid housemaid, until the cost of her air ticket was reimbursed. Her passport was taken from her. She was required to work for the B family on occasion. The B family kept her. Siliadin was made to work seven days a week from 07:30 to 22:30 without a break, save for exceptionally on Sundays to attend mass. She was responsible for childcare and domestic chores. She was not paid (save for one or two occasions). She escaped but returned to the B family on the promise they would regularise her immigration status. Siliadin managed to recover her passport and confided in a neighbour, who reported the B family to the modern slavery committee. The court considered that the criminal-law legislation at the time did not afford practical and effective protection against servitude.

Key Points:

- Servitude.
- Forced labour.
- Domestic Service.
- Systems Duty.

Award: None sought.

Awards for violations of Article 4 and other Articles

England and Wales

OOO, OOA, MTK, RTF v Commissioner of Police for the Metropolis [2011] EWHC 1246 (QB), 20 May 2011

Summary: The claimants alleged that the police infringed their Article 3 and 4 rights in failing to investigate their being trafficked from Nigeria and forced into modern slavery. They were required to work without pay for long hours (between 17 and 22 hours a day) In households in and around London, and subject to physical and emotional abuse by the householders. The abuse included beatings with hands, shoes, rulers, ladles, sticks and other objects. The court concluded that there was a failure to investigate allegations from other complainants, including taking their detailed statements, which would have identified the claimants as victims of trafficking and modern slavery thereby enabling the police to take steps to intervene to protect them. Further, following the complaints of the Claimants, there was no investigation by the police.

An undertaking to investigate was promised 18 months after the initial complaint of the claimants.

Key Points:

- Article 4.
- Investigative Duty.
- Slavery.
- Trafficking.
- Domestic Service.
- Parallel Article 3 claim.

Award: £5,000 per claimant for frustration and anxiety over a period of 12 to 15 months, in respect of both Article 3 and 4.

ECtHR

VCL and AN v United Kingdom (2021) 73 E.H.R.R. 9, 16 February 2021

Summary: Both applicants were discovered, separately, in a cannabis factory. They were under 18 when they were discovered and prosecuted for the production of a Class B drug. They explained they had been brought to the UK illegally, were made to work in the factory, and not able to go out. Both were convicted following guilty pleas. After their convictions, both received decisions concluding there were reasonable grounds for believing they had been trafficked, in contrast to the case by the Crown Prosecution Service ("**CPS**") that they had not been trafficked. The applicants' appeals against conviction and sentence were dismissed. In respect of the first applicant, the court found that there had been a violation of Article 4, because he had been charged with a criminal offence and the CPS had not considered referral through the National Referral Mechanism. The CPS failed to provide adequate reasons for concluding that prosecution was justified considering the Competent Authority's conclusion that the applicant had been trafficked as a child. In respect of the second applicant, the violation of Article 4 arose from allowing the criminal proceedings to proceed when it was apparent the second applicant was a minor, there were reasons to conclude he had been trafficked, and the CPS did not provide clear reasons for its decision to prosecute. The Court of Appeal's reliance on the same reasons was flawed. The CPS's deficient review of the case also rendered the proceedings unfair when considering the duties under Article 6.

Key Points:

- Forced labour.
- Criminal Enterprise.
- Operational Duty.
- Parallel Article 6 breach.

Award: €25,000 (£21,802)[64] awarded to each applicant.

Rantsev v Cyprus and Russia (Application no. 25965/04), 7 January 2010

Summary: The daughter of the applicant, OR, travelled from Russia to Cyprus to work in a cabaret owned by XA, who secured her an artiste visa. XA's brother MA was informed that OA had left the shared residence for workers in XA's cabaret. OR was seen at another cabaret. MA collected her, took her to the police station to allege she was an illegal resident. The police declined to arrest her as an illegal resident and said if MA did not take her then she would be allowed to leave. MA took her. The next morning, she was found dead in the street outside the shared residence with a bedspread hanging from the railings. The court found breaches of Articles 2, 4, and 5. Alleged violations of Article 3 were dealt with under Article 4. The court found breaches of the systemic and operational duties under Article 4. The regime around artiste visas did not afford sufficient protection against trafficking and exploitation. The police did not take reasonable measures to protect OR when there was a credible suspicion that OR was trafficked or exploited. Failures in the investigative process in Cyprus were dealt with by reference to Article 2.

---

64 Exchange rate €1.1467 to £1.

Russia violated the procedural obligation under Article 4 for not investigating how OR came to be trafficked.

Key Points:

- Trafficking.
- Sexual Exploitation.
- Systems Duty.
- Operational Duty.
- Investigative/Procedural Duty.
- Immigration.

Award:

- Cyprus – €40,000 (£35,314) in respect of all violations.
- Russia – €2,000 (£1,766) in respect of the violation of Article 4.[65]

Article 4 alone

Zoletic and others v Azerbaijan (Application no. 20116/12), 7 October 2012

Summary: the applicants were recruited in Bosnia and Herzegovina to work in Azerbaijan as construction workers. On arrival, their passports were removed. No work permits were obtained for them. They worked without pay, were forced to live in spartan accommodation, and were beaten, threatened, fined or detained in a specially designated place if they left the accommodation without special written permission. They remained in Azerbaijan for two years before being returned, in unknown circumstances. The court concluded there were no clear attempts to identify and question the implicated persons. The government had not

65 Exchange rate €1.1327 to £1.

been forthcoming in providing information about the investigation. The failures amounted to a violation of Article 4.

Key Points:

- Forced labour.
- Construction Workers.
- Investigative Duty.

Award: €5,000 (£4,035)[66] to each applicant.

CN v United Kingdom (2013) 56 E.H.R.R. 24, 13 November 2012

Summary: CN travelled to the UK on a false passport, and visa, which were taken from her on arrival. She was made to work, through a company, as a carer. Her pay was kept by the company. She received small amounts. When the family she worked for went on holiday, she contacted the police, but was taken to hospital and eventually sectioned under the Mental Health Act 1983, as she was experiencing psychosis and auditory hallucinations. No attempts were made by the police to investigate the company. The ECtHR referenced the systems duty but arguably the violation concerned the investigative duty on its facts.

Key Points:

- Servitude.
- Trafficking.
- Domestic Service.
- Systems Duty.

Award: €8,000 (£6,431)[67].

CN and V v France (Application no. 67724/09), 11 January 2013

---

66 Exchange rate €1.2393 to £1.

67 Exchange rate €1.244 to £1.

Summary: The applicants were French nationals born in Burundi. Mr and Mrs M had custody of them, following the death of their parents. They were required to undertake domestic chores for the family of nine people, including caring for the disabled son of Mr and Mrs M. They had limited access to hygiene facilities and lived in a poorly heated cellar/basement. They were both subject to physical and verbal harassment and threats to be returned to Burundi. For five years, the first applicant was required to work seven days a week with no breaks, no pay, no access to education, and no time for leisure. The second applicant had been permitted to attend school. Mr and Mrs M were convicted at first instance, but their convictions were overturned on appeal (save for an allegation of violence against the second applicant). The ECtHR considered there were failures in the legislative and administrative framework.

Key Points:

- Forced labour.
- Servitude.
- Domestic Service.
- Systems Duty.
- No breach of the Investigative Duty.

Award: €30,000 (£25,000)[68] to the first applicant alone.

Chitos v Greece (Application no 51637/12), 4 June 2015

Summary: The applicant was forced to pay a fee to end his army service, to pay back the subsistence and training costs incurred during years of training. The ECtHR concluded that requiring the applicant to pay a large amount in full (rather than by instalments), otherwise the sum

68 Exchange rate €1.2 to £1.

would be subject to a large interest rate, to be discharged failed to strike a fair balance between rights and the interests of community.

Key Points:

- Forced labour.
- Army Service.
- Training costs.

Award: €5,000 (£3,603)[69].

LE v Greece (Application no. 71545/12), 21 January 2016

Summary: LE travelled to Greece. Her passport was confiscated. She was forced into prostitution for two years, to pay a fee of €40,000 to free herself from a voodoo spell that she believed had been cast on her and put her and her family in danger. She claimed asylum. LE was then prosecuted for prostitution offences, though she was acquitted. Steps were taken to remove her from Greece. LE complained that the prosecutors had not taken account of essential evidence that she had been a victim of trafficking. Further investigations resulted in the warrants for arrest being issued for the alleged traffickers. The court found there was a violation of Article 4 arising from the initial rejection of LE's complaint was based on an incomplete evidence file, failures to extend the search for the primary suspect, and there were extensive delays in the investigation. Article 6 with Article 13 violation also found for the absence of a right to complain about the length of the procedure.

Key Points:

- Trafficking.
- Sexual Exploitation.
- Investigative Duty.
- Procedural Duty.

---

[69] Exchange rate €1.3879 to £1.

- Parallel Article 6 and 14 claims.

Award: €12,000 (£9,052)[70].

Chowdhury and others v Greece (Application no. 21884/15), 30 March 2017

Summary: the applicants had been trafficked to work in the strawberry fields of Manolada. The employer refused to pay the workers and threatened to kill them if they did not continue working. The situation and conditions in the fields had been publicised in the media and discussed in parliament. When a first group of applicants demanded their wages for work, they were shot at by the employer. Some workers' complaints were not prosecuted because the authorities concluded the workers had delayed in reporting. The employers were not convicted. The workers' claims were rejected by the court on the basis that the workers accepted the conditions of work. The prosecutor refused to lodge an appeal against the court's decision. The ECtHR found there were failures to prevent situations of human trafficking, to protect the victims, to effectively investigate offences and to punish those responsible for trafficking.

Key Points:

- Forced labour.
- Agricultural Workers.
- Operational Duty.
- Investigative Duty.
- Incalculable pecuniary losses.

[70] Exchange rate €1.3257 to £1.

Award: €16,000 (£10,336) for the applicants who had participated in the domestic court proceedings and €12,000 (£7,752) for the other applicants.[71]

TI and Autres v Greece (Application no. 40311/10), 18 July 2019

Summary: The applicants, Russian nationals, alleged consulate employees were bribed by Russian traffickers and issued visas to bring the applicants into Greece for the purpose of sexual exploitation. They were recognised as victims of human trafficking. Criminal proceedings were issued against the people who had directly exploited the applicants, as well as proceedings relating to the issuance of visas. The prosecution of the suspects could not proceed because delays in the investigation resulted in the prosecution being limitation barred. The preliminary investigation lasted three years. The ECtHR found a violation of Article 4 arising from the failures in the investigation, as trafficking between Russia and Greece was well-known, the accusation against state agents and the seriousness of the allegations all required diligent investigation which was not undertaken.

Key Points:

- Trafficking.
- Sexual Exploitation.
- Investigative Duty.
- Procedural Duty.

Award: €15,000 (£13,492)[72].

SM v Croatia (2021) 72 E.H.R.R. 1, 25 June 2020

Summary: SM complained she had been forced into prostitution by a man she had met on Facebook, TM, who had said he knew her parents

---

[71] Exchange rate €1.548 to £1.

[72] Exchange rate €1.1118 to £1.

and offered to help her find a job. TM forced her to provide sex services for payment. TM slapped SM when she had spoken to the first client. TM required SM to provide sexual services every day. He would beat her if she did not. SM complained to the police. TM was charged. TM was acquitted because, though he had organised a prostitution ring, he had not forced or pressured SM into prostitution, which was a constituent element of the local offence. SM complained that there was deficient application of the relevant criminal-law mechanisms. The ECtHR concluded that the prosecuting authorities made no effort to enquire into the contact between SM and TM on Facebook; or to obtain evidence from SM's parents, neighbours, owners of the flat used for prostitution, or other identifiable witnesses. The significant flaws meant the implementation of the criminal law provisions constituted a violation.

Key Points:

- Forced labour.
- Sexual Exploitation.
- Investigatory Duty.
- Procedural Duty.

Award: €5,000 (£4,495)[73].

Krachunova v Bulgaria (2024) 79 E.H.R.R. 6, 28 November 2023

Summary: The applicant moved in with a man, X, after she had argued with her parents. She was asked by him to engage in prostitution. She agreed. She worked daily for between six to nine hours. She wanted to quit but was afraid of X's reaction. She escaped and returned to her home village. X collected her and persuaded her to resume prostitution. She was arrested and interviewed. X attended the police station with her identity card which he said she had given to him. X was convicted of trafficking. The applicant was unable to claim for unpaid wages because the money was earned through "lewd and immoral acts". X was ordered

[73] Exchange rate €1.1123 to £1.

to pay non-pecuniary damages to Krachunova. The Article 4 violation arose from the failure to enable victims of trafficking to claim compensation for pecuniary losses from their traffickers.

Key Points:

- Forced labour.
- Sexual Exploitation.
- Systems Duty.

Award: €6,000 (£5,221)[74].

[74] Exchange rate €1.1492 to £1.

CHAPTER FIVE

ARTICLE 5

1. Everyone has the right to liberty and security of person. No one shall be deprived of his liberty save in the following cases and in accordance with a procedure prescribed by law:

(a) the lawful detention of a person after conviction by a competent court;

(b) the lawful arrest or detention of a person for non-compliance with the lawful order of a court or in order to secure the fulfilment of any obligation prescribed by law;

(c) the lawful arrest or detention of a person effected for the purpose of bringing him before the competent legal authority on reasonable suspicion of having committed an offence or when it is reasonably considered necessary to prevent his committing an offence or fleeing after having done so;

(d) the detention of a minor by lawful order for the purpose of educational supervision or his lawful detention for the purpose of bringing him before the competent legal authority;

(e) the lawful detention of persons for the prevention of the spreading of infectious diseases, of persons of unsound mind, alcoholics or drug addicts or vagrants;

(f) the lawful arrest or detention of a person to prevent his effecting an unauthorised entry into the country or of a person against whom action is being taken with a view to deportation or extradition.

2. Everyone who is arrested shall be informed promptly, in a language which he understands, of the reasons for his arrest and of any charge against him.

3. Everyone arrested or detained in accordance with the provisions of paragraph 1(c) of this Article shall be brought promptly before a judge or other officer authorised by law to exercise judicial power and shall be entitled to trial within a reasonable time or to release pending trial. Release may be conditioned by guarantees to appear for trial.

4. Everyone who is deprived of his liberty by arrest or detention shall be entitled to take proceedings by which the lawfulness of his detention shall be decided speedily by a court and his release ordered if the detention is not lawful.

5. Everyone who has been the victim of arrest or detention in contravention of the provisions of this Article shall have an enforceable right to compensation.

Introduction and principles

1. Prohibition of the imprisonment of a person has long standing roots in the common law. "*Every imprisonment is prima facie unlawful and that it is for a person directing imprisonment to justify his act*" (*Liversidge v Anderson* [1942] AC 206 at 245). Article 5's right to liberty and security of person, setting out the proscribed exemptions and procedural requirements, helpfully reflects the justifications that are also well established in the English and Welsh common law.

2. Domestic scales of damages may be relevant where the violation of the Convention right has an outcome akin to a private law wrong (*Alseran v Ministry of Defence* [2017] EWHC 3289 (QB)).

3. In *R (Lee-Hirons) v Secretary of State for Justice* [2016] UKSC 46, the Supreme Court considered the recall of an individual who had been

conditionally discharged from a hospital and restriction order, in circumstances where the reasons for recall had not been specified. Lord Wilson JSC observed at [46] that "*damages should not be payable to the claimant for the breach of his right under article 5.2 of the Convention any more than that they should be payable for the breach of his right at common law. He has failed to establish that their effects on him were sufficiently grave.*"

4. Generally, where there has been a loss of liberty arising from a failure by authorities to justify the individual's continued detention (by reference to the principles in *R v Governor of Durham Prison, ex parte Singh* [1984] 1 All ER 983), the individual is compensated by reference to the scale of damages in false imprisonment claims (*Thompson v Commissioner of Police of the Metropolis* [1998] QB 498).

5. Accordingly, this chapter limits itself to damages where the awards have been made specifically by reference to a finding that Article 5 has been violated; where the circumstances warranted a separate award in the absence of a claim under the common law; or where the facts justified an award separate to any domestic claim for damages.

6. Awards reflect the importance of the right to liberty, which should not be removed save under the conditions provided for in domestic law and in conformity with the rule of law. However, whilst non-pecuniary damages may be awarded for unlawful detention, in *HL v United Kingdom* (2005) 40 E.H.R.R. 32 the ECtHR confirmed that procedural violations do not normally attract an award of non-pecuniary damages *unless* there had been a delay caused by the procedural failure or where the individual would not have been detained absent the procedural failure.[75]

7. Violations of Articles 5(3) and 5(4) generally attract relatively small non-pecuniary damage awards unless the individual can demonstrate

[75] *Osborn v Parole Board* [2013] UKSC 61 at [2(xiii)].

they would not have suffered the deprivation of their liberty if they had had the benefit of the guarantees of Article 5(3).

8. The award of damages under Article 5(5) depends on proof of damage. In some cases, feelings of distress and frustration has been considered insufficient to require a monetary award but, in other cases, such feelings warranted the award of damages without independent proof. A review of the cases concerning the United Kingdom in the ECtHR demonstrates that the finding of a violation is generally treated as just satisfaction. However, more recent cases have trended towards small awards being made.

Parole[76]

England and Wales

R (Pennington) v the Parole Board [2010] EWHC 78 (Admin), 22 December 2010

Summary: the court concluded that there had been a more than 3-month delay between the date that the defendant should have communicated to the claimant that he should be released from custody and when he was actually told.

Key Points:

- Article 5(4).
- Delay in release.

Award: £1,750.

---

[76] The powers and procedures of the Parole Board have changed over the period of time that these cases were decided. Nevertheless, the awards made for the procedural violations demonstrate the level of awards for delay cross-applicable in respect of current procedures.

Hester v Secretary of State for Justice [2011] EWHC 3926 (Admin), 20 December 2011

Summary: the applicant complained that the defendant had failed to refer his case to the Parole Board timeously after he had been recalled to prison for breach of his licence conditions, namely not living at an approved address or not keeping in contact. He had been unlawfully detained for 12 weeks due to the delay.

Key Points:

- Article 5(4).
- Prison recall.
- Delay in referral.

Award: £6,000.

Haynes v Secretary of State for Justice [2012] EWHC 2481 (QB), 25 July 2012

Summary: the claimant had been recalled to prison for alleged breaches of his licence conditions. He had not been given the reasons for his recall, nor the opportunity to make representations to the Parole Board, immediately following his arrest. He was given the recall representations pack at 12 days after it was due. When the Parole Board considered his representations, the Parole Board released him. His claim alleged violations of Articles 5(2) and (4), 6 and 8. He was awarded damages for the breach of Article 5(2) and a declaration for the breach of Article 5(4).

Key Points:

- Article 5(2).
- Article 5(4).
- Prison recall.
- Delay in reasons.

Award: £1,500.

R (Faulkner) v Secretary of State for Justice and another; R (Sturnham) v Parole Board and another (Nos 1 and 2) [2013] UKSC 23; [2013] UKSC 47, 3 July 2013

Summary: the first case concerned a delay in referring the claimant's case to the Parole Board, which resulted in a 10-month delay in the eventual consideration and release in breach of Article 5(4). In the second case, the claimant was sentenced to an indeterminate term of imprisonment for the public protection. His case was referred to the Parole Board in anticipation of the expiry of his minimum term, but the prison authority's reports were not supplied to the Board timeously, resulting in a delay in the Board's review in breach of Article 5(4). Detention prolonged in breach of Article 5(4) did not amount to false imprisonment, absent exceptional circumstances.

Key Points:

- Article 5(4).
- Delay with evidence.

Award: £6,500 in the first case, bearing in mind the conditional and precarious nature of the liberty foregone. £300 was appropriate in the second case.

R (Haney and others) v Secretary of State for Justice [2014] UKSC 66, 10 December 2014

Summary: the four cases heard by the Supreme Court considered the variety of opportunities that prisoners could be offered to demonstrate their suitability for release, which in turn were argued to have resulted in a delay to the consideration of their release by the Parole Board or a refusal by the Parole Board to recommend less restrictive conditions to demonstrate suitability for release. Only two claimants succeeded. In Haney's case, there was a year-long delay to his transfer to open conditions. In Massey's case, there was a one-year delay to his starting on a course recommended as required for him to demonstrate his suitability for release.

Key Points:

- Article 5(1).
- Article 5(4).
- Ancillary Duty: opportunity to procure release.

Award:

- Haney – £500.
- Massey – £600.

R (Parratt) v Secretary of State for Justice [2014] EWCA Civ 1478, 21 November 2014

Summary: the claimant had been imprisoned for the public protection. They alleged there had been two periods of delay in arranging parole board hearings which gave rise to violations of Articles 5(4) (four months) and delay between two parole board hearings (another 3-month delay). A sum was agreed by the parties if an award did not include an element for loss of liberty. The Court of Appeal eventually accepted that there was an element for loss of liberty which was due to be quantified following further written argument.

Key Points:

- Article 5(4).
- No loss of liberty.
- Delayed independent review.
- Agreed sum.

Award: £250.

R (Guntrip) v Parole Board of England and Wales and Secretary of State for Justice [2014] EWHC 4180 (Admin), 17 December 2014

Summary: the Secretary of State cancelled the claimant's parole board hearing after he had been transferred to a secure unit for psychiatric assessment under the Mental Health Act 1983. The court concluded that: the hearing should have been adjourned, to avoid restarting the process; the decision to cancel had been unilateral; it undermined the Parole Board's independent status; and was premature as the claimant was mid-assessment and could have returned to prison. The cancellation meant that the review took place 17 months later. The delay violated Article 5(4) which was compounded by a further four-month delay caused by administrative errors.

Key Points:

- Article 5(4).
- Delayed independent review.

Award: £2,500 (apportioned 30:70 between the defendants).

R (Knights and O'Brien) v Parole Board of England & Wales and Secretary of State for Justice [2015] EWHC 136 (Admin), 11 February 2015

Summary: the claimants were prisoners subjected to sentences of imprisonment for the public protection. In the second claimant's case, there was a delay of three months in holding a review to consider his release.

Key Points:

- Article 5(1).
- Ancillary duty: opportunity to procure release.
- Delayed independent review.

Award: £300 for delay of 3 months.

R (Kessie-Adjei) v Secretary of State for Justice [2022] EWHC 722 (Admin), 30 March 2022

Summary: The claimant was detained after being unlawfully at large, though his probation officer had not informed the claimant that his licence had been revoked. He had understood his licence had expired and was surprised to have been arrested six months after its anticipated expiry. He was detained for 59 days before he was released by the Parole Board. Although the court did not agree that there was a breach of Article 5(1), the court gave judgment on likely award had the detention been arbitrary.

Key Points:

- Article 5(1).
- Article 5(4).
- Delay in release.
- Miscommunication.
- Claimant culpability.

Award: £5,000 (had the claimant been successful).

<u>ECtHR cases</u>

Curley v United Kingdom (2001) 31 E.H.R.R. 14, 28 June 2000

Summary: the applicant was convicted of murder and was given a tariff sentence of eight years. After his tariff expired, following five separate reviews by the Parole Board, the Parole Board submitted a recommendation for the applicant's release which was rejected by the Secretary of State for Justice who required the applicant to have a trial in a category D (open conditions) prison. The applicant contended that his reviews failed to comply with Article 5(4) because the Parole Board did not have the power to direct release.

Key points:

- Article 5(4).
- No independent power of release.

Award: £1,500.

Oldham v United Kingdom (2001) 31 E.H.R.R. 34, 26 September 2000

Summary: the applicant complained that the two-year delay between his Parole Board reviews was unreasonable, after he had been recalled to prison despite him finishing the rehabilitation work required of him.

Key Points:

- Article 5(4).
- Delay in release.

Award: £1,000.

Hirst v United Kingdom (2006) 42 E.H.R.R. 41, 24 July 2001

Summary: the applicant complained that the review by the Parole Board was not carried out with sufficient expedition, in violation of Article 5(4). His review took place 5 and a half months after the expiry of his tariff and a review every two years was too long. The ECtHR agreed that delays of 21 months and two years between reviews was not reasonable.

Key Points:

- Article 5(4).
- Delay in release.
- Delayed independent review.

Award: £1,000.

Waites v United Kingdom (Application no. 53236/99), 10 March 2003

Summary: the applicant complained that there was a failure to afford him an oral hearing upon his recall to prison. The applicant did not have the opportunity to cross examine witnesses relevant to the allegations that his conduct posed a risk. Though he should have had access to an oral hearing, which amounted to a violation of Article 5(4), he had no enforceable right to compensation.

Key Points:

- Article 5(4).
- No access to independent review.

Award: €2,500 (£1,707)[77].

Von Bülow v United Kingdom (2004) 39 E.H.R.R. 16, 7 January 2004

Summary: the applicant complained that his continued detention beyond his tariff without review by the parole board amounted to a violation of Article 5(4), which the government agreed with.

Key Points:

- Article 5(4).
- No access to independent review.

Award: €1,500 (£1,038)[78].

Hill v United Kingdom (Application no. 19365/02), 27 July 2004

Summary: the applicant complained that he had not had a proper review of his detention following the expiry of his tariff, as the Parole Board had no power to order his release. He was not able to have an oral hearing

---

77 Exchange rate €1.4649 to £1.

78 Exchange rate €1.4447 to £1.

until 10 years after the expiry of his tariff. The ECtHR agreed that the inability of the Parole Board to direct his release (even if they could recommend such) and the inability to examine witnesses violated Article 5(4).

Key Points:

- Article 5(4).
- No access to independent review.
- Delayed independent review.

Award: €2,200 (£1,464)[79].

Blackstock v United Kingdom (2006) 42 E.H.R.R. 2, 21 June 2005

Summary: the applicant complained that the lapse of time between the recommendation for an early review and his actual had been too long, in light of the Parole Board's recommendation that he had an earlier review. The ECtHR concluded there had been a delay of 22 months, which violated Article 5(4).

Key Points:

- Article 5(4).
- Delayed independent review.

Award: €1,460 (£976)[80].

Clift v United Kingdom (Application no. 7205/07), 13 July 2010

Summary: the applicant complained that his continued imprisonment following the recommendation by the Parole Board that he be released on licence breached Article 5 taken with Article 14. The requirement – that prisoners, who were serving a sentence of over 15 years, would only

[79] Exchange rate €1.5023 to £1.

[80] Exchange rate €1.4952 to £1.

be released on approval by the Secretary of State – constituted discrimination. The ECtHR found that the government failed to justify that the difference in treatment was objectively justified.

Key Points:

- Article 5(4).
- Article 14.
- No access to independent review.

Award: €10,000 (£8,362)[81].

James, Wells and Lee v United Kingdom (2013) 56 E.H.R.R. 12, 18 September 2012

Summary: the applicants were imprisoned for the public protection and complained that their post-tariff detention violated Article 5(1). They argued the failure to offer the means of rehabilitation allowing them to demonstrate a reduction in their alleged risk levels, which was the basis of their continued detention, rendered the detention arbitrary. The ECtHR accepted that the applicants' continued detention was a consequence of the risk they were perceived to post and the lack of availability of courses to demonstrate a reduction in their perceived risk rendered their detention arbitrary and unlawful.

Key Points:

- Article 5(1).
- Ancillary duty: opportunity to procure release.

Award:

- James – €3,000 (£2,395) for 5 months.
- Wells – €6,200 (£4,950) for 21 months.

---

81 Exchange rate €1.1959 to £1.

- Lee – €8,000 (£6,389) for 30 months.[82]

Betteridge v United Kingdom (2013) 57 E.H.R.R. 7, 29 January 2013

Summary: the applicant complained about the delay of almost 13 months in his case being heard by the Parole Board, which had been found to be unlawful by the High Court.

Key Points:

- Article 5(4)
- Delayed independent review.

Award: €750 (£625)[83].

Detention following arrest

Steel and others v United Kingdom (1999) 28 E.H.R.R. 603, 23 September 1998

Summary: the applicants were arrested after attending protests. The first applicant had been detained for 44 hours, the second for 17 hours, and the third to fifth for 7 hours. The first and second applicants refused to be bound over and were committed to prison for 28 days and 7 days respectively. They alleged their arrests and periods in police detention violated Article 5(1) because "breach of the peace" was not sufficiently certain under English law. In respect of the third, fourth and fifth applicants, the ECtHR concluded that their detention for approximately 7 hours was unlawful because it could not find any evidence that the

82 Exchange rate €1.2524 to £1.

83 Exchange rate €1.2 to £1.

applicants' protest had been anything other than peaceful. The court also found their Article 10 rights had been violated.

Key Points:

- Article 5(1).
- Protest.
- Parallel Article 10 claim.
- Police detention.

Award: £500 to the third, fourth and fifth applicants.

Caballero v United Kingdom (2000) 30 E.H.R.R. 643, 8 February 2000

Summary: the applicant claimed that the automatic denial of bail by statute, due to his arrest on suspicion of attempted rape, amounted to a violation of his Article 5(3) rights. The government accepted that he had had good prospects of bail had it not been for the statutory restriction on granting bail for those charged with attempted rape. The applicant was eventually convicted of attempted rape.

Key Points:

- Article 5(3).
- Blanket Approach.
- Bail.
- Claimant culpability.

Award: £1,000.

Allen v United Kingdom (2010) 51 E.H.R.R. 22, 30 March 2010

Summary: the applicant complained that the requirements of Article 5(3) were not complied with as the decision maker could not give a binding ruling on bail, because the prosecution could appeal. Additionally, the applicant was not permitted to attend the hearing of the prosecution's appeal against bail, which violated her Article 5(4) rights. The ECtHR considered that the applicant should have had the same procedural guarantees as in the original bail hearing and she should have been able to attend the hearing, the failure amounted to a violation of Article 5(4).

Key Points:

- Article 5(4).
- Blanket Approach.
- Bail.

Award: €1,000 (£902)[84].

Mentally disordered

England and Wales

R (KB and others) v Mental Health Review Tribunal (Damages) [2003] EWHC 193 (Admin), 13 February 2003

Summary: the claimants were all patients detained under the Mental Health Act 1983, who had experienced delays in the hearing of their applications to challenge their detention. The delays amounted to an infringement of their rights to a speedy hearing as protected by Article 5(4) and all were entitled to damages.

Key Points:

- Article 5(4).
- Delayed independent review.
- Mental Health detention.

---

[84] Exchange rate €1.1092 to £1.

Awards:

- PD: £1,000 – three cancelled hearings and three-week delay. No evidence of injury to PD's health resulting from the delay in the hearing of his application. No specific evidence of distress or frustration.
- KB: £0 – short delay of two and a half weeks and no evidence of injury to KB's health.
- LB – £0 – discharged by responsible clinician before the hearing could be listed, as a listing could not be confirmed due to the lack of availability of a medical member. There was less than 50% prospects LB would have been discharged earlier, if her tribunal hearing had taken place.
- GM – £1,000 – four cancellations and 11-week delay. The delay had caused distress to GM, but there was no prospect of him being discharged earlier.
- JR – £4,000 – four cancellations and 12-week (+) delay. Contemporaneous medical evidence that JR experienced prolonged frustration with cancellations from the tribunal that he did not experience with other cancellations. A significant chance that JR may have been discharged in one of the tribunal hearings that was cancelled.
- MK – £1,000 – four and a half weeks' delay. MK was unnecessarily detained for two further weeks and was required to remain in a minimum secure ward rather than an open ward owing to the delayed discharge.
- TB – £750 – three cancellations and 13-week delay. There was no evidence of injury to TB's health. No specific evidence of distress or frustration. No expectation of a conditional discharge.
- B – £1,000 – multiple adjournments, 6-month delay. B was not discharged.

Neary v London Borough of Hillingdon [2011] EWHC 1377 (CoP), 9 June 2011

Summary: Requiring a 21-year-old man with autism and a severe learning disability to live in a support unit for 12 months, rather than letting him return home with his father, amounted to an unlawful deprivation of his liberty. The local authority failed to appoint an independent mental capacity advocate; failed to ensure an effective review under the Mental Capacity Act 2005; and had failed to issue proceedings timeously. The court concluded that had these failings not occurred, the claimant would have returned earlier than he did.

Key Points:

- Articles 5(1) and 5(4).
- Parallel Article 8 claim.
- Delayed independent review.
- Delayed access to representative.
- Settlement.

Award: £35,000.[85]

A Local Authority v D and another (Case no. 12140104), 10 July 2013

Summary: The court approved a settlement agreement made on behalf of a protected party ("**Mrs D**") for damages agreed following the local authority's admission that it had violated Mrs D's Article 5 and 8 rights by failing to ensure that Mrs D's detention had been reviewed speedily by a court between August 2011 and April 2012 (as the application issued did not indicate that Mrs D objected to her detention) and/or failure to ensure that interference with Mrs D's contact with her husband (where he was prevented from taking Mrs D home) was necessary and proportionate. A declaration was made that Mrs D had been unlawfully

---

[85] The award was referenced in *A Local Authority v D and another* (Case no. 12140104) but the judgment itself does not refer to the sum agreed.

deprived of her liberty between 5 May 2012 and 26 September 2012. The claim settled without admission in respect of Mrs D's detention between August 2011 and April 2012.

Key Points:

- Article 5(1).
- Article 5(4).
- Parallel Article 8 claim.
- Delayed independent review.
- Settlement.

Award: £15,000 to Mrs D and £12,500 to Mrs D's husband.

Bostridge v Oxleas NHS Foundation Trust [2015] EWCA Civ 79,[86] 10 February 2015

Summary: the claimant was unlawfully detained for 442 days following his recall under a community treatment order, that was technically flawed because a person could not be placed on a community treatment order if they had been discharged by a tribunal. The claimant's detention had been reviewed on two occasions after he return to hospital. It was considered the claimant required continued detention.

Key Points:

- Article 5(1).
- Legal error.
- Hospital recall.

Award: None. No greater than nominal award was necessary by way of "just satisfaction".

---

86 Often the case is compared with the outcome in *Esegbona v King's College Hospital NHS Foundation Trust* [2019] EWHC 77 (QB) but that case did not concern a claim for a violation of Article 5.

ECtHR

Johnson v United Kingdom (1999) 27 E.H.R.R. 296, 24 October 1997

Summary: the applicant was remanded for an assault he caused when he was suffering from a mental illness. The applicant complained that his deferred conditional discharge violated Article 5(1)(e) because he was no longer of unsound mind. The court accepted that deferring discharge may fall within the margin of appreciation offered to states but such deferral could not be indefinite. The imposition of a hostel residence condition resulted in an infinite deferral of the applicant's discharge and the delay violated Article 5(1)(e). The delay in the applicant's case was 3.5 years.

Key Points:

- Article 5(1)(e).
- Blanket Approach.
- Delay in release.

Award: £10,000.

Hutchison Reid v United Kingdom (2003) 37 E.H.R.R. 9, 20 February 2003

Summary: the applicant complained that his detention in hospital, based on his diagnosis of anti-social personality or psychopathic disorder, violated Article 5(1) in the absence of any possibility or intention of provision of medical treatment. There had been a violation of Article 5(4) due to the delay of three months and eleven days in his review. The ECtHR concluded that there must be some relationship between the grounds of detention and the place and condition of detention. Although the ECtHR concluded there was no violation of Article 5(1), there had been a violation of Article 5(4) because the burden of proof was on an individual to establish his detention was unlawful, which was not compatible with Article 5(4).

Key Points:

- Article 5(4).
- Burden of proof.
- Delayed independent review.

Award: €2,000 (£1,340)[87].

Committal

Northern Ireland

Magennis v Northern Ireland Courts and Tribunals Service [2022] NIQB 6, 27 January 2022

Summary: on two occasions, the claimant had failed to pay fines which resulted in warrants being issued for him to serve 7-days' imprisonment. The warrants had been issued pursuant to a process that was held to be unlawful.

Key Points:

- Article 5(1).
- Warrant Process.
- Parallel Article 6 claim; no award.

Award: £5,000 for each 7-day period of imprisonment, in the absence of any evidence of the impact on the claimant.

---

87 Exchange rate €1.4924 to £1.

ECtHR

Beet v United Kingdom (2005) 41 E.H.R.R. 23, 6 July 2005

Summary: the applicants were found liable to pay local taxes by a magistrates' court or had been fined by a court following a criminal conviction. Each applicant did not pay the fine. Non-payment was due to wilful refusal or neglect. The applicants were sentenced to a period of imprisonment, suspended on the condition they would make payments. Their failure to pay meant that their term of term of imprisonment was activated. They were all imprisoned. Free legal representation was not available for the enforcement proceedings at the relevant time and none of the applicants were legally represented at the hearings in front of the magistrates. There had not been an inquiry into the ability of the applicants to pay the fines, which vitiated the order for committal. The magistrates' order was made in excess of its jurisdiction and amounting to violations of Articles 5(1) and Article 5(5). There was a commensurate finding that Article 6(1) had been violated.

Key Points:

- Article 5(1).
- Article 5(5).
- Fines.
- Parallel Article 6 claim; no award.
- Claimant culpability.

Award: €5,000 (£3,437)[88] in the case of Beet.

Lloyd and others v United Kingdom (Application no. 29798/96 and others), 6 July 2005

Summary: the applicants argued that they had been committed to prison in circumstances where they had failed to pay their taxes. The applicants

---

[88] Exchange rate €1.4547 to £1.

argued their committal had failed to comply with Article 5(1) because: the magistrates had not considered alternatives to imprisonment; the process had not ensured there was opportunity for under-21-year-olds to be represented; or the magistrates had not been satisfied that they had received proper notice of the hearing. The highest awards were given to the following applicants:

- Kane, who spent 4 days in prison, but her family did not know where she was, underwent a strip search and has been unable to sleep, and had been on medication since.

- Massey, who was 60 years old and spent 5 days in prison.

- Pitt, who spent 4 days in prison and her young children had to be left in unsatisfactory care arrangements. She has since suffered from anxiety.

- Lisa Watts, who spent 7 days in prison and was unable to contact her family.

- Lloyd, who spent 36 days in prison.

- Barker, who spent 28 days in prison.

Key Points:

- Article 5(1).
- Fines.
- Limited evidence of harm.

Award:

- €6,000 (£4,125) – Kane; Massey; and Pitt.
- €7,000 (£4,812) – Lisa Watts.
- €9,000 (£6,187) – Lloyd and Barker.

- €5,000 (£3,437) for the others.[89]

Military Custody

England and Wales

Alseran and others v Ministry of Defence [2017] EWHC 3298 (QB), 14 December 2017

Summary: Various claims by Iraqi civilians for unlawful imprisonment and ill-treatment during the United Kingdom's participation in the military action in Iraq from 2003 to 2009. The Article 5 claims related to the following periods of detention:

- Alseran: 27 days.
- MRE: six days.
- KSU: six days.
- Al-Waheed: 33 days.

Key Points:

- Article 5.
- Parallel Article 3 claim.
- Initial detention lawful.
- Delay in release (in respect of Al-Waheed).

Awards: Day rate of £100 used, because detention was initially lawful.

- Alseran: £2,700.
- MRE: £600.
- KSU: £600.
- Al-Waheed: £3,300.

[89] Exchange rate €1.4547 to £1.

ECtHR

Al-Jedda v United Kingdom (2011) 53 E.H.R.R. 23, 7 July 2011

Summary: the applicant had been arrested in Iraq by US forces and then transferred to the custody of British forces for over three years.

Key Points:

- Article 5(1).
- Internment – no justification under Article 5(1) relied on.
- Military.

Award: €25,000 (£22,108)[90].

Immigration

England and Wales

M v Secretary of State for the Home Department [2011] EWHC 3667 (Admin), 6 December 2011

Summary: the claimants were asylum seekers that the Secretary of State for the Home Department ("**SSHD**") had intended to remove to Germany, pursuant to the then Dublin Convention. Action was not taken to remove them for six years. Following the issue of a warrant, the claimants were detained in their home and removed to Germany within six hours. The SSHD accepted the removal was unlawful. Damages were calculated by reference to domestic legal principles for false imprisonment.

Key Points:

- Article 5.

90 Exchange rate €1.1308 to £1.

- Parallel Article 8 claim.
- Damages for common law claim.
- Unlawful Removal.
- Order returning the family to the UK.

Award: £4,500 to each claimant.

<u>Northern Ireland</u>

Re Jokubauskas's Application for Judicial Review [2017] NIQB 45, 2 May 2017

Summary: the applicant was deported because he had committed drug offences. His removal was delayed because there had been a delay in obtaining his travel documents and the SSHD did not have his Home Office file. The award was made to recognise that he had been detained three days longer than he should have been.

Key Points:

- Article 5.
- Delay in removal.

Award: £1,500.

<u>ECtHR</u>

A v United Kingdom (2009) 49 E.H.R.R. 29, 19 February 2009

Summary: the applicants were subject to restrictive measures in the UK, following the terrorist attacks committed by Al-Qaeda and the inability of the UK to deport them. Derogations from Article 5 had been submitted by the UK government. Their certification and the associated restrictions on their liberty were considered by the Special Immigration Appeals Commission ("**SIAC**"). The ECtHR found that there had been violations of Article 5(1) as the derogation measures had been disproportionate; the measures discriminated between nationals and non-nationals. There had been a violation of Article 5(1) in respect of all but two of the applicants. In respect of four applicants, there had been a violation of Article 5(4) because the evidence in the open material was not sufficiently specific for the detainees to provide meaningful instructions to the special advocates for the SIAC procedure to comply with procedural aspects of Article 5(4). The damage was:

- First Applicant – lost his liberty for 3 years and 83 days, and experienced mental illness.
- Third Applicant – lost his liberty for three and a half years, with mental illness and distress to his family.
- Fifth Applicant – lost his liberty for 2 and a half years, and house arrest on release, with mental illness.
- Sixth Applicant – lost his liberty for three years and three months, with suffering and distress to his family.
- Eighth applicant – lost his liberty for two and a half years, with mental suffering and distress and concern to move to avoid media attention.
- Ninth applicant – lost his liberty for 2 years and 11 months, suffered mental illness, and distress to family.
- Tenth applicant – lost his liberty for 2 years and 2 months, with mental illness.
- Eleventh Applicant – lost his liberty for one year and six months.

Key Points:

- Article 5(1).
- Article 5(4).
- Terrorism.

Award:

- €3,900 (£3,462) for the first, third and sixth applicants.
- €3,400 (£3,018) for the fifth applicant.
- €3,800 (£3,374) for the seventh applicant.
- €2,800 (£2,486) for the eighth applicant.
- €3,400 (£3,018) for the ninth applicant.
- €2,500 (£2,219) for the tenth applicant.
- €1,700 (£1,509) for the eleventh applicant.[91]

Abdi v United Kingdom (2013) 57 E.H.R.R. 16, 9 April 2013

Summary: the applicant complained that his detention was not compatible with Article 5(1)(f) because immigration removals to Somalia were not possible, or in the alternative his detention was not in accordance with the law as there had been a failure to conduct regular reviews of his detention. He was detained for two years and four months. The court considered that, for all practical purposes, the claimant's removal had become virtually impossible and so his detention was no longer affected with a view to his deportation which amounted to a violation of Article 5(1).

Key Points:

- Article 5(1).
- Immigration detention.
- Delay in removal.

Award: €1,500 (£1,276)[92].

[91] Exchange rate €1.1264 to £1.

[92] Exchange rate €1.175 to £1.

JN v United Kingdom (Application no. 37289/12), 19 May 2016

Summary: the applicant argued that the domestic law concerning immigration detention lacked the quality of law. The absence of fixed time limits and lack of automatic judicial oversight were unjustified. The ECtHR disagreed but found that the lack of diligence by the authorities for over a year amounted to a breach of Article 5(1)(f).

Key Points:

- Article 5(1).
- Immigration detention.
- Delay in removal.

Award: €7,500 (£5,838)[93].

VM v United Kingdom (2017) 64 E.H.R.R. 7, 1 September 2016

Summary: the applicant complained that her detention in immigration detention was unlawful because she was mentally ill and there was no realistic prospect of removal.

She was detained for nearly two years. The court concluded that there was a violation of Article 5(1) as the authorities had not acted with due diligence for a period of seven months between VM's fresh representations and the decision made, against the backdrop of a long period detention and her deteriorating mental health.

Key Points:

- Article 5(1).
- Immigration detention.
- Delay in decision.
- Mental Health.

---

93 Exchange rate €1.2846 to £1.

Award: €3,500 (£2,986)[94].

[94] Exchange rate €1.1722 to £1.

CHAPTER SIX

ARTICLE 6

1. In the determination of his civil rights and obligations or of any criminal charge against him, everyone is entitled to a fair and public hearing within a reasonable time by an independent and impartial tribunal established by law. Judgment shall be pronounced publicly but the press and public may be excluded from all or part of the trial in the interest of morals, public order or national security in a democratic society, where the interests of juveniles or the protection of the private life of the parties so require, or to the extent strictly necessary in the opinion of the court in special circumstances where publicity would prejudice the interests of justice.

2. Everyone charged with a criminal offence shall be presumed innocent until proved guilty according to law.

3. Everyone charged with a criminal offence has the following minimum rights:

(a) to be informed promptly, in a language which he understands and in detail, of the nature and cause of the accusation against him;

(b) to have adequate time and facilities for the preparation of his defence;

(c) to defend himself in person or through legal assistance of his own choosing or, if he has not sufficient means to pay for legal assistance, to be given it free when the interests of justice so require;

> *(d) to examine or have examined witnesses against him and to obtain the attendance and examination of witnesses on his behalf under the same conditions as witnesses against him;*
>
> *(e) to have the free assistance of an interpreter if he cannot understand or speak the language used in court.*

Introduction

1. Article 6 ensures that everyone, in the determination of their civil rights and obligations, or of any criminal charge against them, shall enjoy a fair and public hearing within reasonable time by an independent and impartial tribunal established by law. There are additional rights connected with criminal charges.

2. As observed by Lord Bingham in *R (Greenfield) v Secretary of State for the Home Department* [2005] UKHL 14, it does not follow from an Article 6 violation that the outcome of the trial process was wrong or would have been different, had the breach not occurred. In 2005, when *Greenfield* was decided, Lord Bingham observed that, in the vast majority of Article 6 cases before the ECtHR, the finding of a violation was itself just satisfaction. Where an Article 6 violation is discovered, the outcome will often be that the court's decision is quashed, and a retrial ordered.

3. The court has been willing to depart from its practice, that the finding of a violation is just satisfaction to remedy a breach of Article 6, where there is a causal connection between the violation identified and the losses for which the applicant claimed to be compensated.[95] Where there have been excessively long proceedings, there is a strong, but rebuttable, presumption that such length will necessitate an

[95] *R (Greenfield) v Secretary of State for the Home Department* [2005] UKHL 14 at [11].

award for non-pecuniary damage.[96] When awards have been made, they have been for relatively small amounts.

4. The most prevalent line of cases where damages have been awarded were in the family courts. In *Medway Council v T* below, the parties agreed that the factors to be taken into account in cases where there was a breach or breaches of Articles 6 and 8, the relevant factors to take into account were:

    a. length of the proceedings;

    b. length of the breach severity;

    c. distress caused;

    d. involvement of the child or parent in decision making; and

    e. any other procedural failings.

5. It is necessary to observe that there have been fewer reported cases, where non-pecuniary damages for breaches of Article 6 have been awarded in family cases in recent years. It may be due to a decision in respect of the impact of the legal aid framework on these awards. The awards in these cases should be treated with some caution as damages have generally been awarded for dual breaches of Article 6 and Article 8 without clear delineation.

Criminal Proceedings

Perks and Others v United Kingdom (1999) 30 E.H.R.R. 33, 12 October 1999

Summary: the applicants, who were dependent on state benefits or low income, had been imprisoned for failures to pay a community charge

---

96 *Apicella v Italy*, (Application no. 64890/01), 29 March 2006, at [93].

(poll tax). They were charged for the failure to pay poll tax and were detained on conviction. The sentences were quashed by the High Court. By the time the case got to the ECtHR, it was common ground that there had been a violation of Article 6(1) and 6(3)(c), in that the applicants had no right to legal aid and were not legally represented, in circumstances where they lacked funds to pay for legal representation. The court awarded non-pecuniary damages to Mr Perks alone, because the High Court judge found as fact that it was unlikely that Mr Perks would have been committed to prison had the magistrates known about his health problems and personal circumstances.

Key Points:

- Article 6(1).
- Article 6(3)(c).
- No legal aid.
- Violation conceded.
- Different outcome likely.

Award: £5,500.

Allan v United Kingdom (2003) 36 E.H.R.R. 12, 5 November 2002

Summary: the applicant's rights pursuant to Articles 6, 8 and 13 were violated by the covert recording of him in his cell, in the prison visiting area, and of his alleged admission to a fellow prisoner, and the use of this material in his trial for murder, impinging his right to silence and his privilege against self-incrimination. In awarding damages, the court considered that the applicant's rights had been violated in multiple ways. The applicant must have felt frustration and an invasion of his privacy, which would not be vindicated by the finding of a violation alone.

Key points:

- Article 6(1).
- Right to silence.
- Covert recordings.

- Criminal prosecution.

Award: €1,642 (£1,046)[97].

Mellors v United Kingdom (2004) 38 E.H.R.R. 11, 17 July 2003

Summary: three years and two weeks for the applicant's appeal against his conviction to be determined amounted to an unreasonable length of proceedings, even though the appeal had been dismissed. The ECtHR concluded the claimant had experienced some distress and frustration due to the length of proceedings.

Key Points:

- Article 6(1).
- Delay in proceedings.
- Claimant culpability.

Award: €2,800 (£1,961)[98].

VCL and AN v United Kingdom (2021) 73 E.H.R.R. 9, 5 July 2021

Summary: Both applicants were discovered, separately, in a cannabis factory. They were under 18 when they were discovered and prosecuted for the production of a Class B drug. They explained they had been brought to the UK illegally, were made to work in the factory, and not able to go out. Both were convicted following guilty pleas. After their convictions, both received decisions concluding there were reasonable grounds for believing they had been trafficked, in contrast to the case by the Crown Prosecution Service ("**CPS**") that they had not been trafficked. The applicants' appeals against conviction and sentence were dismissed. The CPS's deficient review rendered the proceedings unfair and incompatible with Article 6. The Court of Appeal's narrow role of

---

97 Exchange rate €1.5694 to £1.

98 Exchange rate €1.4277 to £1.

review penalised victims of trafficking for not identifying themselves as victims. Appeal did not cure the defects by the CPS. The ECtHR concluded that the Article 6(1) violations were essentially procedural in nature and as such the ECtHR did not consider the merits of the prosecutorial decisions. There was a parallel finding that Article 4 had been violated (dealt with in Chapter 4).

Key Points:

- Article 6(1).
- Forced labour.
- Criminal Enterprise.
- Procedural errors.
- Parallel Article 4 breach.

Damages: €25,000 (£21,410) awarded to each applicant (for both breaches).[99]

Civil Proceedings

Hammerton v United Kingdom (2016) 63 E.H.R.R. 23, 17 March 2016

Summary: the applicant was committed to prison for three months for contempt of court, following the alleged breach of an undertaking that he would not personally contact or communicate with his former wife, her parents or her solicitors. The Court of Appeal had quashed the finding of contempt of court due to procedural errors by the county court (failing to enquire why the applicant had not been represented and failing to adjourn to allow him to obtain representatives). The Court of Appeal concluded his sentence would have been far shorter had he been represented. The ECtHR found that there had been a lack of effective remedy in not being able to claim damages for the violation of Article

99 Exchange rate €1.1677 to £1.

6(1) and Article 6(3)(c) due to the applicant's inability to obtain representation.

Key Points:

- Article 6(1).
- Article 6(3)(c).
- Legal Representation.
- Different outcome likely.

Award: €8,400 (£6,558)[100].

Family Proceedings

<u>England and Wales</u>

Re H (A Child: Breach of Convention Rights: Damages) [2014] EWFC 38, 29 October 2014

Summary: The local authority admitted poor practice through the course of care proceedings, which the court concluded had an inevitable adverse impact on the parents. The local authority accepted it failed to explore the parents' capacity to consent to the H's placement promptly; it had failed to issue proceedings in a timely manner; failed to involve parents in decision making; placed insufficient weight on the parents' wish to care for H; and failed to explain the options to the parents.

Key Points:

- Article 6.
- Delay in assessments.
- Delay in proceedings.
- Parallel Article 8 claim.

---

[100] Exchange rate €1.2809 to £1.

- Breach admitted.

Award: £6,000 for each parent.

Northamptonshire County Council v AS and others [2015] EWHC 199 (Fam), 30 January 2015

Summary: the claimant was placed with foster carers with his mother's consent, but it took five months for the local authority to make the decision to start care proceedings, and a further three and a have months to take the step to issue proceedings, without any explanation for the delay. There was a failure to: undertake assessments of the child's family members; undertake case planning; and comply with court orders. The local authority conceded violations of Article 6 and 8.

Key Points:

- Article 6.
- Delay in proceedings.
- Delay in assessment.
- Failure to comply with court orders.
- Parallel Article 8 claim.
- Breach admitted.

Award: £12,000 for the child and £4,000 for the mother.

Re AS (A Child) (Unlawful removal) [2015] EWFC B150, 7 August 2015

Summary: the local authority failed to issue proceedings in a timely manner after it had removed the child, without the mother's consent or judicial authority, into its care when the mother had been admitted to hospital under the Mental Health Act 1983 when her mental health had relapsed. The local authority had failed to comply with a strict time limit of bringing the removal before the court within 72 hours for an emergency protection order.

Key Points:

- Article 6.
- Removal of child.
- Mental health.
- Delay in proceedings.

Award: £3,000.

Medway Council v T (Case No. ME15C00859), 13 October 2015

Summary: the local authority had accommodated the child for over two years. It had failed to obtain the mother's consent or an order of the court. The local authority did not bring proceedings as soon as the child was accommodated. The local authority conceded that it had failed to establish the mother's capacity to challenge the accommodation of the child; there was little consideration of the child's legal status; there was a lack of management oversight; and there were significant delays in facilitating contact and ensuring access to support for the child. The mother and child were unable to remedy their relationship when the mother was in better mental health. The mother provided evidence from her treating psychiatrist, though the court could not conclude that her mental health deteriorated by the failures of the local authority.

Key Points:

- Article 6.
- Removal of child.
- Delay in proceedings.
- Parallel Article 8 claim.
- Breach admitted.
- Expert evidence.

Award: £20,000 to both the child and mother (for both breaches).

X, Y, Z v West Sussex County Council (Case no. SD15C00558), 23 February 2016

Summary: the local authority was found to not have requisite authority to make decisions on behalf of the children, including authority to refuse contact between the children and their mother, breaching the children's Article 8 rights. The local authority: failed to issue care proceedings for two and a half years, leaving the children without access to independent representation and remedy; delayed assessment of the children; and had failed to carry out assessment of the children's mother. The independent reviewing officer did not progress the case. The factors the court considered relevant to the children's damages award: length of delay before assessment; denied access to independent legal representation; little promotion of contact with mother (especially for 12 months after the child expressed a desire to speak to mother); frequent placement changes without input from anyone with parental responsibility; placement with placing with foster carers without assessment and not being in culturally appropriate placements. The important features in the mother's damages award were her frequent but ignored requests for contact and the failure to assess her. However, it was unlikely the children would have been placed with her if she had been assessed timeously.

Key Points:

- Article 6.
- Delay in proceedings.
- Delay in assessment.
- Legal representation.
- Parallel Article 8 claim.

Award: £20,000 to each child and £5,000 to the mother (for both breaches but observed to be mostly for the Article 8 breach).

Worcestershire County Council v Mother and The Child (Case No. WR15Z00014), 29 January 2016

Summary: the local authority failed to make an application to revoke a placement order, and the independent reviewing officer took no action to progress the revocation over three years. The local authority conceded breaches of Article 6 and 8. Damages were awarded due to the length of time involved and the severity of the breaches of the child's rights, taken together with the impact of such breaches in the form of his loss of access to justice and the lost opportunity, over three years, to develop a relationship with at least one of his half siblings. The loss of a chance also took into account of the child's behavioural issues and mother's parenting limitations.

Key Points:

- Article 6.
- Delay in proceedings.
- Parallel Article 8 claim.
- Breach admitted.

Award: £5,000 (for both breaches).

Kent County Council v M and K [2016] EWFC 28, 13 May 2016

Summary: the court found that there was a failure of the local authority to conduct or update the core assessment for over three years, meaning that there was no secure foundation for care planning whilst the child was placed with the local authority. The local authority failed to secure appropriate mental health assessments of the children and/or therapeutic support which meant the child's placement breakdowns were unsupported. The local authority failed to provide an opportunity to secure a suitable long-term placement for the children. The local authority had failed to act on its own decisions for over three years and failed to issue proceedings earlier.

Key Points:

- Article 6.
- Delay in assessment.
- Delay in proceedings.
- Parallel Article 8 claim.

Award: £17,500.

GD and BD (by their Children's Guardian), MD and FD v Wakefield Metropolitan District Council and another [2016] EWHC 3312 (Fam), 20 December 2016

Summary: the children were removed from their mother's care, following the arrest of their parents on suspicion of involvement in the downloading and distribution of indecent images of children. Both the local authority and police force admitted breaches of Article 6 and 8, and the sum awarded was agreed by all the parties. The conceded breaches of Article 6 were: failing to disclose conversations between the local authority and police about key evidence; failing to update the court that one of the offending video clips emanated from USA (including failing to ensure it was referenced in the police's statement); failing to pursue more specific orders for disclosure into the family proceedings; failing to disclosure the existence of evidence; failing to send the same evidence to the expert ABE (Achieving Best Evidence) interviewer with the children were flawed; failing to respond to detailed requests for information with information that had been in the LA's possession; the opening note of the LA did not record at all/accurately the entirety of the relevant evidence; and the allegations against mother were maintained until final hearing when the allegation should have been withdrawn months earlier.

Key Points:

- Article 6.
- Failure to disclose key evidence.
- Failure to comply with court orders.

- Parallel Article 8 claim.
- Breach admitted.
- Agreed sums.

Award: £10,000 to the mother and £5,000 for each child.

Thurrock Borough Council v W & B (Case no. CM15C05449), 27-29 June 2016

Summary: The local authority violated the child's Article 6 and 8 rights by: failing to issue proceedings for thirteen months; failed to establish contact between her and her mother or her siblings for over a year; and failed to arrange for therapy.

Key Points:

- Article 6.
- Delay in proceedings.
- Parallel Article 8 claim.
- Breach admitted.

Award: £7,500.

AZ and others v *Kirklees Council* [2017] EWFC 11, 16 February 2017

Summary: the local authority conceded that it violated the claimants' Article 6 rights in failing to inform them of an urgent hearing and – when they were not in attendance – informing the court that they had been so notified.

Key Points:

- Article 6.
- Failure to give notice.
- Misrepresentation to court.
- Parallel Article 8 claim.
- Breach admitted.

Award: £3,750 to each claimant.

ECtHR

H v United Kingdom (1991) 13 E.H.R.R. 449, 9 June 1988

Summary: Article 6 had been violated by the failure of the local authority, for 5 months, to notify parties of adoption placement proceedings. The delay in proceedings violated Article 8 because there was an interference with the opportunities of the applicant to develop a relationship with her child.

Key Points:

- Article 6(1).
- Delay in proceedings.
- Parallel Article 8 claim.

Award: £12,000.

McMichael v United Kingdom (1995) 20 E.H.R.R. 205, 24 February 1995

Summary: the applicants' child was removed from them and made available for adoption. The failure to disclose confidential reports and other documents to the applicants in advance of the children's placement hearings, resulted in decisions taken by the court in relation to the applicants and their child that failed to afford the applicants' requisite protection of their rights under Articles 6 and 8.

Key Points:

- Article 6(1).
- Removal of child.
- Failure to disclose key evidence.
- Parallel Article 8 claim.

Award: £8,000 (jointly).

P, C, & S v United Kingdom (2002) 35 E.H.R.R. 31, 16 July 2002

Summary: the local authority removed the child from his mother and made available for adoption, because the local authority was concerned that the mother had Munchhausen's syndrome and previously had been convicted in the USA for deliberately administering laxatives to her older son, endangering his life. The failure to provide the mother with the assistance of a lawyer, where such assistance was indispensable due to the complexity of the proceedings and where the proceedings were emotionally challenging. The court also found breaches of Article 8 for the removal of the child shortly after birth and failing to involve the mother in the decision-making process.

Key Points:

- Article 6(1).
- Removal of child.
- Parallel Article 8 claim.
- Legal representation.

Award: €12,000 (£7,660) for both mother and child (for both breaches).[101]

---

[101] Exchange rate €1.5665 to £1.

CHAPTER SEVEN

ARTICLE 7

1. No one shall be held guilty of any criminal offence on account of any act or omission which did not constitute a criminal offence under national or international law at the time when it was committed. Nor shall a heavier penalty be imposed than the one that was applicable at the time the criminal offence was committed.

2. This Article shall not prejudice the trial and punishment of any person for any act or omission which, at the time when it was committed, was criminal according to the general principles of law recognised by civilised nations.

Introduction

1. Rarely referenced, but logically grouped with Articles 5 and 6, Article 7 effectively protects against retrospective punishment. The finding of a violation of Article 7 usually constitutes sufficient just satisfaction, when considered alone (*Kafkaris v Cyprus* (2009) 49 E.H.R.R. 35). The few limited cases make clear, as in many areas of the Strasbourg jurisprudence, that the position is not fixed. When a claim pursuant to Article 7 is grouped with alleged violations of other Convention rights, the likelihood of a monetary award for non-pecuniary damages depends on the default position in relation to the other Articles in the group.

2. There is little domestic case law that deals with Article 7 violations. This chapter looks exclusively to the ECtHR.

No award

Welch v United Kingdom (1995) 20 E.H.R.R. 247; (1996) 21 E.H.R.R. CD1, 26 February 1996

Summary: The applicant was found guilty of possession with intent to supply cannabis and cocaine and convicted on five counts, receiving a 22-year sentence. Between being charged for the cannabis offenses and cocaine offences and being convicted, the Drug Trafficking Offences Act 1986 came into force. The sentencing judge imposed a confiscation order pursuant to that Act. The ECtHR concluded that the confiscation order amounted to a penalty of a punitive character, which were more far-reaching than the applicant was exposed to at the time of the commission of the offences. Accordingly, there had been a violation of Article 7, but the confiscation order had not been enforced at the time of the hearing.

Key Points:

- Confiscation Order.
- Change: new penalty introduced.
- Non-enforcement of the penalty.

Award: None.

Article 7 alone

Gurguchiani v Spain (Application no. 16012/06), 15 December 2009

Summary: The applicant was convicted of burglary and sentenced to 18 months' imprisonment. The court was asked to expel the applicant from the country, in place of a prison sentence, as he was a Georgian citizen living illegally in Spain. The first instance court refused to expel the applicant. The prosecutor appealed. The criminal code changed to mandate an expulsion order as opposed to a prison sentence where an illegal immigrant was given a prison sentence of up to six years. The court decided to replace the sentence of imprisonment with an expulsion order where the applicant could not return to Spain for 10 years. The replacement of the prison sentence with an expulsion order without the prospect of re-entering lawfully for 10 years exceeded the potential expulsion order that could have been considered at the time of the original sentence (and which the court had not then made). It was therefore a more severe penalty than previously provided for under the previous criminal code.

Key Points:

- Article 7 violation alone.
- Change: available sentences.
- Criminal proceedings and immigration.

Award: €5,000 (£4,494)[102].

Camilleri v Malta (2013) 57 E.H.R.R. 32, 22 January 2013

Summary: The applicant was charged with possession of ecstasy not for his own use. He alleged the ability of the prosecuting authority to determine the forum of his trial (and accordingly the maximum available sentence) violated Article 6. If tried under the Medical and Kindred Professions Ordinance (concerning the investigation, trial and punishment of offences involving psychotropic drugs) in the Court of Magistrates, the maximum sentence was ten years, but in Criminal Court the maximum sentence was life imprisonment. The applicant was tried in the Criminal Court and was sentenced to 15 years' imprisonment. The law did not determine with precision the circumstances in which a punishment bracket applied. The prosecuting authority had, in effect, unfettered discretion to decide which punishment bracket would be applicable, leaving room for arbitrariness. By failing the foreseeability

[102] Exchange rate €1.1127 to £1.

requirement and lack of effective safeguards against arbitrary punishment, there was a violation of Article 7.

Key Points:

- Article 7 violation alone.
- Legal provision failed to have the necessary quality of foreseeability.
- Legal provision failed to have effective safeguards in place.

Award: €1,000 (£833)[103].

Awards for violations of Article 7 and other Articles

Scoppola v Italy (2010) 51 E.H.R.R. 12, 17 September 2009

Summary: The applicant had been convicted for murdering his wife and injuring his son. He elected to be tried by a summary procedure, that had not been available to him at the time he committed the offence, but did become available after charge. The summary procedure limited the maximum sentence to 30 years' imprisonment on conviction. He elected the summary procedure on that basis. By the date his sentence was handed down, the law had changed to increase the maximum sentence that could be imposed in the summary procedure to life imprisonment. The prosecution appealed the imposition of a 30-year sentence successfully. The ECtHR concluded that, even though he faced the prospect of life imprisonment at the time he committed the offence, he had elected the summary procedure based on the legal position at the time (and waived the right to a public trial on that basis), the penalty was therefore heavier than prescribed by law.

103 Exchange rate €1.2 to £1.

Key Points:

- Parallel Article 6 claim.
- Change: maximum sentence.

Award: €10,000 (£8,919)[104].

Del Rio Prada v Spain (2014) 58 E.H.R.R. 37, 21 October 2013

Summary: The applicant was convicted for terrorism offences. The combination of the applicant's sentences amounted to over 3,000 years, but the convicting court fixed the maximum sentence of 30 years' imprisonment and any remissions of the sentence for work done in detention would be deducted from that maximum penalty. Her proposal to the national court, for remissions to her sentence, was rejected due to changed legislation that remissions could not be considered by reference to the maximum term of imprisonment imposed but, rather, by reference to each successive individual sentence. The ECtHR emphasised that the concept of a penalty does not exclude measures introduced after the pronouncement of sentence, and thus the domestic court's departure from the discernible consequence of the pre-existing legal position amounted to a violation of Article 7.

Key Points:

- Parallel Article 5 claim.
- Prison remissions to reduce sentence length.
- Change: calculation of sentence requirements.

Award: €30,000 (£25,430)[105].

---

[104] Exchange rate €1.1212 to £1.

[105] Exchange rate €1.1797 to £1.

M v Germany (2010) 51 E.H.R.R. 41, 10 May 2010

Summary: The applicant had an extensive criminal history for offences involving theft and/or serious assault. He had escaped from prison four times. When he was convicted of attempted murder and robbery, assault, and blackmail, he was sentenced to 5 years' imprisonment and subject to preventative detention, which – at the time of its making – was limited to 10 years following his prison sentence. Whilst in the preventative detention period of imprisonment, the criminal code change to extend the maximum period of preventative detention to an unlimited period. Due to his conduct in prison and his previous convictions, his preventative detention was extended. The ECtHR found that the potential indefinite duration of preventative detention, when coupled with the absence of complementary measures to support prisoners subject to preventative detention orders, made the applicant subject to additional detention three times the length of his original sentence. The preventative detention was a heavier penalty than prescribed by law at the time of his sentence.

Key Points:

- Parallel Article 5 claim.
- Change: term of imprisonment.

Award: €50,000 (£42,790)[106].

Glien v Germany (Application no. 7345/12), 28 November 2013

Summary: The applicant had been convicted for sexual offences against children. He complained that his preventative detention been extended unlawfully due to a change in the criminal law that could extend the period of preventative detention retrospectively. Article 5(1) was violated because the preventive detention was not justified as the detention of a person of unsound mind for the purposes of Article 5(1)(e). Preventative

106 Exchange rate €1.1685 to £1.

detention was indistinguishable from a prison sentence and amounted to a heavier penalty in violation of Article 7.

Key Points:

- Parallel Article 5 claim.
- Change: term of imprisonment.

Award: €3,000 (£2,513)[107].

WA v Switzerland (2022) 74 E.H.R.R. 13, 2 February 2022

Summary: the applicant had been convicted of murder and intentional manslaughter and sentenced to 20 years' imprisonment. The sentencing court decided not to order further preventative detention due to the likely short duration of a further preventative detention. Upon serving his sentence, the prosecuting authority placed him in detention whilst applying for preventative detention of the applicant, pursuant to the change of the criminal code, which reopened the proceedings. The court ordered the applicant's preventative detention. The detention of the applicant in an ordinary prison, as opposed to a psychiatric facility rendered his detention a breach of Article 5(1)(e). The additional term of imprisonment was a heavier penalty imposed retrospectively.

Key Points:

- Parallel Article 5 claim.
- Change: term of imprisonment.

Award: €40,000 (£33,520)[108].

---

[107] Exchange rate €1.1938 to £1.

[108] Exchange rate €1.1933 to £1.

CHAPTER EIGHT

ARTICLE 8

1. Everyone has the right to respect for his private and family life, his home and his correspondence.

2. There shall be no interference by a public authority with the exercise of this right except such as is in accordance with the law and is necessary in a democratic society in the interests of national security, public safety or the economic well-being of the country, for the prevention of disorder or crime, for the protection of health or morals, or for the protection of the rights and freedoms of others.

Introduction

1. The breadth of case law under Article 8 fairly reflects the breadth of the concepts of private and/or family life, which makes pinpointing principles on the award of damages for violations thereof markedly challenging in comparison to other Convention rights. Its full scope is the right to respect for one's private life, family, home and correspondence. Article 8 can encompass infringements of privacy in the usual sense, as well as infringements of bodily integrity and is frequently cited in claims against public authorities.

2. Where the general principles require practitioners to look at the practice in the award of damages by reference to each Article, when one considers Article 8, it is further necessary to look at the courts' practice in respect of particular aspects of private and/or family life. Accordingly, in this chapter, it is vital to understand the cases where the finding of violation or declaration has been considered sufficient just satisfaction.

3. Immediately after the commencement of the HRA, the courts looked to the decision in *R (on the application of Bernard) v Enfield London Borough Council* [2002] EWHC 2282 (Admin) for guidance on appropriate awards for Article 8 where there had been maladministration, which in turn considered the awards for redress made by the Local Government Ombudsman. In respect of maladministration, where a public authority takes steps to remedy a situation, little or no award at all was considered sufficient.

4. The competing interests of Article 8 and Article 10 has given rise to extensive discussion, which in turn formed the foundation of claims between private individuals, known as "misuse of private information" claims (a tort for the purposes of service (*Vidal-Hall and others v Google Inc* [2015] EWCA Civ 311). This chapter would not be complete without reference to some of the awards made pursuant to that cause of action, even though it is often relied on with other claims, for instance: defamation, breaches of the data protection act, and/or breach of confidence.

5. Factors such as actual (as opposed to assumed) distress/damage, bad faith, malice, award of damages for common law claims, and the claimant's conduct play more prominent roles in the consideration of whether a non-pecuniary award is required for just satisfaction.

Immigration

<u>England and Wales</u>

R (on the application of Mambakasa) v Secretary of State for the Home Department [2003] EWHC 319 (Admin), 3 March 2003

Summary: The claimant was a refugee from Angola, who arrived in the UK in 1996, and was granted asylum and indefinite leave to enter as a refugee in 2001. The claimant's family was eventually granted entry clearance to join him in 2002, but the process had been littered with delays and administrative errors. Although the court found that there had been an unreasonable delay of six months, there had not been a violation of Article 8. The court nevertheless opined on the likely award of damages had there been a violation.

Key points:

- Family life.
- Family separation.
- Delay.
- Maladministration.

Award: None. Had the court found a breach of Article 8, the court would have awarded £1,000 – £2,000.

R (Shaw and others) v Secretary of State for the Home Department [2013] EWHC 42 (Admin), 18 January 2013

Summary: The removal of the claimants was not in accordance with the law, as the claimants were not given any opportunity to seek access to justice. There was a parallel claim for unlawful detention. By the time of this judgment, the claimants had already been brought back to the UK and had their immigration applications reconsidered (although they were refused again). The court assessed the claimants' claim for damages for unlawful detention and a breach of Article 8. The court awarded £2,000 each for 10 hours of false imprisonment and determined that a separate award for just satisfaction for breach of Article 8 was not necessary. Therefore, a declaration of breach was sufficient in the circumstances of this case.

Key points:

- Immigration removal.
- Private life.
- Access to justice.
- Damages for common law claim.

Award: None.

ECtHR

Omojudi v United Kingdom (App. No. 1820/08), 24 February 2010

Summary: The applicant was deported to Nigeria following his convictions for sexual offences. He had lived in the UK for 26 consecutive years. His deportation caused the separation of him from his wife and children, who could not reasonably have been expected to move to Nigeria with him. The adverse impact on his family from his deportation violated Article 8 and warranted an award for non-pecuniary damages.

Key points:

- Deportation.
- Family life.

Award: €3,000 (£2,628)[109].

A.W Khan v United Kingdom (App. No. 47486/06), 12 April 2010

Summary: The applicant was a Pakistani national and had been in the UK since he was three years old. He was convicted of a drugs offence. The Secretary of State made a deportation order. The ECtHR concluded that the decision to deport him violated his Article 8 rights, on the basis of: his time spent in the UK; the lack of ties to Pakistan; and his lack of reoffending since he had been released from prison. The applicant did not seek damages.

Key points:

- Deportation.
- Family life.

---

[109] Exchange rate €1.1415 to £1.

- No request for damages.

Award: None.

AA v United Kingdom (App. No. 8000/08), 20 December 2011

Summary: The applicant was a Nigerian national, who had been convicted of a rape that he had committed two years after arriving in the UK when he was a minor. He had since settled in the UK and progressed through to university. He committed no further offences, no steps had been taken to deport him for seven years, and he was assessed as being of a low risk of reoffending. The court held that the applicant's deportation breached his Article 8 rights. No award was made because the applicant did not request an award.

Key points:

- Deportation.
- Private life.
- No request for damages.

Award: None.

Hode and Abdi v United Kingdom (2013) 56 E.H.R.R. 27, 6 February 2013

Summary: The refusal to allow a refugee's spouse to join him in the UK, because he had married his spouse after he had arrived in the UK, violated both the refugee and his spouse's family life. There was no justification for the difference in treatment. The fact that the applicants were denied the opportunity to spend the first years of their marriage living together, and the impact on the first applicant's opportunity to bond with his first child, were relevant to the valuation of the award.

Key points:

- Spousal reunification.
- Family life.
- Parallel Article 14 claim.

Award: €6,000 (£5,175)[110].

Unuane v United Kingdom (2021) 72 E.H.R.R. 24, 24 February 2021

Summary: Deporting the applicant after he had been convicted of obtaining money transfer by deception breached his right to family life, as he was separated from his wife and children, one of whom had a congenital heart defect. The seriousness of the offence did not outweigh the best interests of his children.

Key Points:

- Immigration removal.
- Family life.
- Family separation.
- Criminal offending.

Award: €5,000 (£4,360)[111].

---

110 Exchange rate €1.1594 to £1.

111 Exchange rate €1.1467 to £1.

Housing and Home

England and Wales

R (on the application of Bernard) v Enfield LBC [2002] EWHC 2282 (Admin), 25 October 2002

Summary: The social services department at Enfield Council undertook an assessment of Mrs Bernard's needs, as she was severely disabled after a stroke. They concluded that her accommodation was not suitable to meet her needs but failed to find suitable accommodation for the claimant. Mrs Bernard brought a claim that the Council had breached her Article 8 and Article 3 rights by leaving her in unsuitable accommodation for 20 months. The High Court concluded that there was no breach of Article 3, but that the council's housing department's delay, after the receipt of its social services' department's report, had violated the claimant's Article 8 rights. The court found this case to be an extreme example of maladministration as: (i) there was a serious breach of the claimants' Article 8 rights; (ii) the conditions that the family had to live in were "deplorable" and inimical to an ordinary family life; (iii) there had been a negative impact on Mrs Bernard's physical and psychological integrity for an extended period of time; (iv) the council had been urged to take action by the claimants' solicitors on a number of occasions and did not do so; (v) the housing department had threatened to evict the claimants; and (vi) there had been no explanation or apology. Just satisfaction required a monetary award, even though the claimants had been provided with suitable accommodation and rent security by the date of judgment. There was no comparable tort that could be a useful reference for quantum and, instead, the court took into account the Local Government Ombudsman's awards.

Key points:

- Adequacy of housing.
- Private and family life.
- Delay.

- Duties to disabled people.
- Aggravating conduct by council.

Award: £8,000 for Mrs Bernard and £2,000 for Mr Bernard.

Dennis v Ministry of Justice [2003] EWHC 793 (QB), 16 April 2003

Summary: The claimants brought a claim in nuisance and for breach of their Article 8 rights complaining about the noise from RAF fighter planes operating near their home. The court concluded that the noise did amount to a nuisance but accepted that there was a public interest in the continued training of RAF pilots. The court also held that there was an interference with the claimants' rights under Article 8. The court awarded damages in nuisance for £950,000. The court held that this award was sufficient just satisfaction and no further award was necessary. However, the judge opined that, had he needed to make a separate award for a breach of Article 8, in respect of the second claimant then, he would have awarded £20,000 but he would have reduced the damages award for nuisance accordingly.

Key points:

- Nuisance.
- Private life.
- Damages for common law claim.

Award: None. In the alternative, the court would have awarded £20,000 (had there been no award for nuisance).

Andrews v Reading Borough Council [2005] EWHC 256 (QB), 7 February 2005

Summary: The claimant brought a claim against his local council after changes to the roads near his home, including the diversion of traffic, led to increased noise pollution. The court held that there was a breach of the claimant's Article 8 rights. The court stated that if the Council had offered a portion of the costs incurred by the claimant for installation of double glazing, then it would be unlikely that any court would have awarded any damages. However, since no such offer was made by the Council in this case, the court considered it appropriate to make a damages award.

Key points:

- Noise pollution.
- Private life.
- Conduct by council.

Award: £2,000.

Dobson v Thames Water Utilities Ltd [2011] EWHC 3253 (TCC), 8 December 2011

Summary: The claim against the defendant company was for private nuisance, negligence, and a breach of their Article 8 rights, arising out of the operation of a nearby sewage treatment plant. The court held that the defendant did breach the claimants' Article 8 rights. The court considered the loss of amenity was compensated for in the award of damages in respect of the nuisance claim (in total £20,120 between 15 claimants) and also vindicated by, amongst other things, a declaration. On that basis, taking into account the principles applied by the ECtHR, it was not necessary to afford just satisfaction to make an award of damages to the residents, who did not have a proprietary interest.

Key points:

- Nuisance.
- Private life.
- Damages for common law claim.

Award: None.

Clift v Slough Borough Council [2009] EWHC 1550 (QB), 6 July 2009

Summary: The claimant was placed on the local authority's "Violent Persons Register", which was shared with other public authorities. In his libel, data protection, and Article 8 claim, the court found that the council had a defence to the libel claim insofar as it had shared information with other departments in its own council, but the sharing of information to other public authorities was not proportionate or fair. The jury awarded damages of £12,000 in respect of the libel claim. The court concluded that the declaration made the award of damages for a breach of Article 8 unnecessary.

Key points:

- Libel.
- Data protection.
- Private life.
- Use of registers.
- Damages for common law claim.

Award: None.

R (on the application of Y) v Secretary of State for the Home Department [2013] EWHC 4141 (Admin), 20 December 2013

Summary: The claimant was an Algerian national who had been given Indefinite Leave to Remain but became subject to deportation proceedings on national security grounds. The claimant was subject to strict bail conditions to remain in a house on the outskirts of Bedford pending the conclusion of the deportation proceedings. The claimant complained that he was suffering negative mental health due to the isolation of living in Bedford. The delay of two months to find the claimant suitable accommodation after a medical report confirmed an adverse impact on the claimant violated the claimant's Article 8 rights.

Key points:

- Adequacy of housing.
- Private life.
- Unpublished policies.

Award: £500.

TM (Kenya) v Secretary of State for the Home Department [2017] EWHC 2267 (Admin), 27 July 2017

Summary: The claimant's application to renew her leave to remain in the UK was refused and she was detained in an immigration removal centre. Although her "removal from association" amounted to a breach of her Article 8 rights, the court declined to make an award for damages on the basis that the period of unjustified detention was short (less than four hours) and during the day.

Key points:

- Immigration detention.
- Segregation.
- Private life.
- Declaration.

Award: None.

R (on the application of TMX) v London Borough Council of Croydon [2024] EWHC 129 (Admin), 26 January 2024

Summary: The claimant was an asylum seeker, who suffered with multiple sclerosis and other conditions, which caused extreme physical pain. The claimant was left sharing an en suite bedroom with his wife and two children for seven months, while the local authority and Secretary of State disagreed on which public authority was responsible for the claimant's housing needs. No damages awarded as they had not been sought.

Key points:

- Adequacy of housing.
- Private life.
- Delay.
- Duties to disabled people.

Award: None.

ECtHR

Connors v United Kingdom (2005) 40 E.H.R.R. 9, 27 August 2004

Summary: The applicant and his family were evicted from a local authority caravan site. This was based on alleged antisocial behaviour, but the reasons for the eviction were not given to the applicant. The lack of procedural safeguards in the process of summary eviction were found to have violated the applicant and his family's Article 8, 6, 13 and 14 rights.

Key points:

- Eviction.
- Family life.
- Procedural violation.
- Parallel Articles 6, 13, and 14 claims.

Awards: €14,000 (£9,375)[112].

---

[112] Exchange rate €1.4933 to £1.

McCann v United Kingdom (2008) 47 E.H.R.R. 40, 13 August 2008

Summary: The choice of the housing authority, to bypass the statutory scheme to evict the claimant by asking his ex-partner to sign a common law notice to quit, lacked procedural safeguards. As a result, there had been a breach of Article 8. The award of non-pecuniary damages took into account that: (i) it was a procedural violation; (ii) allegations of domestic violence against the applicant; (iii) that the applicant was a single man (although he wanted contact with his children); and (iv) that it was unclear whether the outcome would have been different if the correct procedure had been followed.

Key points:

- Eviction.
- Private life.
- Procedural violation.

Award: €2,000 (£1,586)[113].

Kay and Others v United Kingdom (2012) 54 E.H.R.R. 30, 21 December 2010

Summary: The occupiers of local authority properties had not been permitted to argue that possession proceedings started by the local authority amounted to a disproportionate violation of their Article 8 rights because they were not direct tenants of the local authority. The inability of the occupiers to rely on Article 8 to defend possession proceedings was incompatible with the safeguards in Article 8 to ensure a proportionality assessment would be undertaken. The award of damages reflected: (i) the procedural nature of the violation and (ii) that it was not clear that the possession order would not have been made, had

113 Exchange rate €1.2614 to £1.

the process been different. Non-pecuniary damages were awarded to acknowledge the applicants' feelings of frustration and injustice.

Key points:

- Eviction.
- Private life.
- Procedural violation.

Award: €2,000 (£1,695)[114] to each applicant.

Buckland v United Kingdom (2013) 56 E.H.R.R. 16, 18 December 2012

Summary: The applicant was a traveller and a possession order was made against her pitch. The ECtHR held that the applicant did not have any possibility to have the proportionality of her eviction determined by a tribunal, and therefore there had been a breach of Article 8. The ECtHR held that the inability of the applicant to challenge the eviction led to feelings of frustration and injustice, although such feelings were mitigated when the County Court suspended the order for up to twelve months.

Key points:

- Eviction.
- Private life.
- Procedural violation.

Award: €4,000 (£3,562)[115].

---

[114] Exchange rate €1.1802 to £1.

[115] Exchange rate €1.1231 to £1.

Employment

<u>ECtHR</u>

Roche v United Kingdom (2006) 42 E.H.R.R. 30, 19 October 2005

Summary: The failure to offer the applicant, a former soldier, an effective and accessible procedure to access information about the toxic gas tests carried out on him in Porton Down, to assess the risk that he had been exposed to toxic chemicals from those tests, amounted to a breach of Article 8. The ECtHR concluded that: he was subject to tests that amounted to military weapons; he had been unwell for some time; the response to his request for disclosure was gradual and incomplete; and he would have felt frustration, uncertainty and anxiety at the failures to provide him access to the information requested.

Key points:

- Delayed disclosure.
- Private life.
- Exposure to toxic chemicals.
- Physical harm.

Award: €8,000 (£5,452)[116].

SW v United Kingdom (2021) 73 E.H.R.R. 18, 22 September 2021

Summary: In an ex-tempore, oral, bullet-point judgment in family court proceedings concerning the determination of allegations of sexual abuse of children, the judge criticised the social worker, SW, for instigating the investigation, lying to the court, and subjecting one of the children to emotional abuse in her interaction with them. No prior notice had been given to SW of the criticisms. The judge rejected the application to anonymise SW in the judgment. The local authority terminated their engagement of SW because of the judge's findings and referred her to her

116 Exchange rate €1.4674 to £1.

regulator. SW was unable to obtain work elsewhere. The Court of Appeal concluded that the process, by which the judge arrived at his criticisms, was manifestly unfair and contrary to the requirements of Article 8 and the common law. SW was unable to bring a claim domestically because she would have been required to establish a lack of good faith, on the part of the judge who made the original comments, which was unlikely. As she did not have effective remedy before a national authority, her Article 13 rights were also infringed.

Key Points:

- Allegations of misconduct.
- Private life.
- Parallel Article 13 claim.

Award: €24,000 (£20,571).[117]

Family and Relationships

<u>England and Wales</u>

C (A Child) [2007] EWCA Civ 2; [2007] EWCA Civ 98, 3 January 2007

Summary: The local authority breached the claimant's Article 8 rights by abandoning a care plan to rehabilitate her with her child, without engaging her in the decision-making process. The court held that the council's breach had been a procedural one and that the distress and outrage felt by the claimant seemed to stem from the removal of her child rather than the procedural breach. The court held that the declaration finding a violation of her rights was sufficient just satisfaction in these circumstances.

---

[117] Exchange rate €1.1667 to £1.

Key points:

- Family Proceedings.
- Removal of child.
- Family life.

Award: None.

R (MG) v Secretary of State for the Home Department [2015] EWHC 3470 (Admin), 3 December 2015

Summary: The claimant established a breach of his Article 8 rights arising out of his accommodation having been placed miles away from where his child lived, without provision for payment of the costs for his travel to see his child. The court declined to award damages because there was no denial of contact between the claimant and his child, only a failure of the state to come to his aid. The claimant's character was also relevant to the decision on damages; the court referred to the claimant's conviction for a serious sexual offence and that he had spent a lot of his limited income on smoking rather than travelling to see his child.

Key points:

- Separation of family.
- Family life.
- Claimant conduct.

Award: None.

CH (by his litigation friend, the Official Solicitor) v A Metropolitan Council [2017] EWCOP 12, 28 July 2017

Summary: CH had been married to WH for five years, before the local authority assessed that CH lacked capacity to consent to sexual relationships. WH was advised that she must abstain from sexual intercourse with CH. The psychologist advised that CH undertake a course of sex education, which the local authority failed to implement until CH's sister issued proceedings on his behalf; a delay of a year and three months from when conjugal relations were required to cease. The education course was delivered in early 2017 and in March 2017, the expert concluded that CH had capacity to consent to sexual relations. The judge observed that an award in excess of £20,000 would have been justified but approved the agreed amounts.

Key Points:

- Spousal relations.
- Family life.
- Mental Capacity.
- Settlement.

Award: £10,000.

Brennan and others v City of Bradford Metropolitan District Council and another (Case no. E22YJ102), 29 January 2021

Summary: The claimants contended that the failure to freeze their family member's body resulted in the body becoming badly decomposed, making it unfit for viewing. This was incompatible with the claimants' Article 8 rights. The knowledge of their family member's extensive decomposition caused them psychological damage. Damages were awarded to acknowledge the strong family ties. The claimants adduced expert evidence that they had been psychologically affected by the decomposition.

Key points:

- Preservation of deceased's body.
- Private and family life.
- Close family ties.
- Expert evidence.

Award:

- Brennan – £2,500.
- L Clarke – £1,000.
- T Clarke – £1,000.
- R Clark – £1,000.
- Leader – £1,000.
- Saia – £1,000.

Bell v Commissioner of the Police of the Metropolis [2024] EWHC 379 (KB), 21 February 2024

Summary: The police had removed the claimant's son's passport from his ex-partner to prevent the son's abduction. The ex-partner said they wanted to take the son abroad for a holiday. Inexplicably, the police returned the son's passport to the ex-partner. They did not ensure that commensurate protective measures, to prevent the abduction of the claimant's son, were put in place. The ex-partner removed the claimant's son from the UK. The claim was made in negligence and pursuant to the HRA. The court held that the police did not take "the necessary steps" to ensure effective protection of the claimant's Article 8 rights and did not ensure that the legal and administrative "scheme" that had been set up to prevent child abduction was "operated competently so as to achieve its aim."

Key points:

- Child Abduction.
- Family life.
- Parallel negligence claim.
- Damages for common law claim.

Award: £28,000.

Scotland

MB v Principal Reporter [2021] CSOH 19, 16 February 2021

Summary: The petitioner was the older brother of four sisters, all of whom were made subject to Compulsory Supervision Orders on the basis that they were related to an individual guilty of relevant offences under the Sexual Offences (Scotland) Act 2009. There was a breach of the petitioner's Article 8 rights because he was deprived of his right to participate in the matter and the previous court had failed to take his interests into account. The court held that a declarator was sufficient to afford the petitioner just satisfaction on the basis that, although there was some unfairness in the procedure of one hearing, for which a breach of Article 8 was established, the unfairness of the procedure did not have the effect of depriving the that deprived the petitioner of contact with his siblings.

Key points:

- Family proceedings.
- Family life.
- Representation.

Award: None.

F v Moray Council [2024] SAC (Civ) 27, 24 November 2023

Summary: The pursuers and respondents in this appeal were foster carers and the children that they had fostered. The foster carers decided to send the children to private school, funded by the monies received by the carers for the fostering services, to help provide the children structure. The placement broke down as a result of the "egregious conduct" of the council's employees, including a prejudice against the decision to send the children to private school. The council threatened to remove the children with notice or preparation for transition. Minutes of the meetings wrongly vilified the carers and made unfounded allegations against them. One child was removed to a residential home despite both the child and the carers wanting the child to stay with the carers. A false allegation of sexual impropriety was made against one carer. Pecuniary losses totalled approximately £195,000.

Key points:

- Family proceedings.
- Family life.
- Foster carer and child relationships.
- Breach admitted.

Award: £8,000.

<u>ECtHR</u>

Dudgeon v United Kingdom (1982) 4 E.H.R.R. 149, 22 October 1981

Summary: The claimant was a homosexual man who brought a challenge under Article 8 and Article 14 against laws in Northern Ireland that criminalised certain sexual acts between consenting adult males. The ECtHR held that the criminalisation of homosexual acts between consenting adult males amounted to an unjustified interference with the claimant's right to respect for his private life under Article 8. The relevant laws in Northern Ireland had, by the time of the decision, been changed to bring them in line with the rest of the United Kingdom and the ECtHR determined that this was sufficient to afford just satisfaction.

Key points:

- Sexual orientation.
- Private life.
- Criminalising homosexuality.

Award: None.

Smith and Grady v United Kingdom (2000) 29 E.H.R.R. 493, 27 December 1999

Summary: Both applicants were administratively discharged from the armed forces because of their homosexuality. The applicants, and people close to them, had been subjected to interviews, asking about details of their sex lives and other personal matters. This amounted to a breach of the applicants' rights under Article 8; neither the investigation into the applicant's homosexuality, nor their discharge was justified under Article 8(2). Non-pecuniary damages were awarded to recognise the grave interferences with their rights, the particularly intrusive and offensive nature of the interview questioning, and the impact on their careers. All of which were found to have had a significant emotional and psychological impact on the applicants.

Key points:

- Sexual orientation.
- Private life.
- Punishment of homosexuality.

Award: £19,000 per claimant.

ADT v United Kingdom (2001) 31 E.H.R.R. 33, 31 October 2000

Summary: In 1996, the applicant was convicted of gross indecency between men (contrary to section 13 of the Sexual Offences Act 1956) following the discovery of videotapes depicting sexual acts between the applicant and other consenting adult men. The ECtHR held that there was no justification for the maintenance of a legislative provision that criminalises homosexual acts between men in private.

Key points:

- Sexual orientation.
- Private life.
- Criminalising homosexuality.

Award: £10,000.

TP and KM v United Kingdom (2002) 34 E.H.R.R. 2, 10 May 2001

Summary: The applicants were a mother ("TM") and daughter ("KM"). KM was removed from TM's care until the local authority's application for wardship was withdrawn some years later. The ECtHR held that there had been a breach of the applicants' Article 8 rights (and Article 13 rights), because the disclosure of a video interview of the child and/or transcript of the interview had not been prompt and deprived TM an effective opportunity to deal with the allegations that her daughter could not be returned safely to her care and deprived her of an adequate involvement in the decision-making process concerning the care of her daughter. KM was not returned to TM for a year. They both suffered distress and anxiety and feelings of injustice.

Key points:

- Care proceedings.
- Family life.
- Removal of child.
- Information sharing with parents.

Award: £10,000 to each applicant.

Beck, Copp and Bazeley v United Kingdom (App. Nos. 48535/99, 48536/99, 48537/99), 22 January 2003

Summary: The applicants brought a claim for breach of Article 8 (and Articles 3, 10, 13 and 14) following an investigation into their sexuality and their discharge from the military on that basis, as a result of the absolute policy against the presence of homosexuals in the military. The investigation process was particularly intrusive; the discharge of the applicants had a profound effect upon them and their careers; and the absolute and general character of the policy led to the discharge of the applicants on the grounds of an innate personal characteristic irrespective of their conduct or service records. The ECtHR adjusted for inflation, as the awards was based on those made in *Smith and Grady* above.

Key points:

- Sexual orientation.
- Private life.
- Criminalising homosexuality.

Award: €30,300 (£19,908)[118] to each applicant.

Perkins and R v United Kingdom (App. Nos. 43208/98 and 44875/98), 22 January 2003

Summary: The applicants alleged that their rights under Article 8 had been violated because of an investigation into their sexuality and their subsequent discharge from the Royal Navy on the basis of their homosexuality due to the absolute policy, that was in existence at the time, against the presence of homosexuals in the armed forces. The investigation process was particularly intrusive; the discharge of the applicants had a profound effect upon them and their careers; and the absolute and general character of the policy led to the discharge of the applicants on the grounds of an innate personal characteristic irrespective of their conduct or service records.

Key points:

- Sexual orientation.
- Private life.
- Criminalising homosexuality.

Award: €30,300 (£19,908)[119] per applicant.

---

[118] Exchange rate €1.522 to £1.

[119] Exchange rate €1.522 to £1.

B.B v United Kingdom (2004) 39 E.H.R.R. 30, 7 July 2004

Summary: The applicant contacted the police after he was attacked by a man, with whom he had sexual relations. He was charged with homosexual sexual activity with a male aged 16, despite the activity being consensual, due to the different ages of consent for homosexual and heterosexual acts. The existence of legislation giving rise to different ages of consent based on sexual orientation violated the applicant's rights under Article 14 read with Article 8.

Key points:

- Sexual orientation.
- Private life.
- Criminalising homosexuality.

Award: €7,000 (£4,660)[120].

Dickson v United Kingdom (2008) 46 E.H.R.R. 41, 4 December 2007

Summary: The applicants were a married couple. The husband was in prison at the time of the application serving a life sentence. The applicants had applied for artificial insemination facilities, as they wanted to have children. Their application was refused by the Secretary of State. The applicants brought a claim alleging that the refusal of artificial insemination facilities amounted to a breach of their rights under Article 8 and Article 12.

The ECtHR held that the policy that applied for artificial insemination facilities, "*set the threshold so high against them from the outset that it did not allow a balancing of the competing individual and public interests and a proportionality test by the Secretary of State or by the domestic courts in their case, as required by the Convention*". Therefore, there was a breach of Article 8. The award was made on the basis that the UK did not

[120] Exchange rate €1.5023 to £1.

adequately consider the interests of the applicants on a matter that was vitally important to them and the failure had been, and continued to be, distressing for the applicants.

Key points:

- Access to artificial insemination facilities.
- Family life.
- Prison law and public policy.
- Parallel Article 12 claim.

Award: €5,000 (£3,607)[121] in total (not split between applicants).

A.D & O.D v United Kingdom (2010) 51 E.H.R.R. 8, 16 June 2010

Summary: O.D (a baby) was found to have bone fractures in the months following his birth. A.D (the mother) suggested that this could have been the result of osteogenesis imperfecta, brittle bone disease. The local authority did not accept the explanation and started care proceedings. O.D was removed from the care of A.D. After O.D sustained a fall whilst in care, the conclusion was that O.D did suffer from osteogenesis imperfecta. A.D brought proceedings in negligence and personal injury on behalf of herself and O.D. The ECtHR held that there had been a breach of Article 8 in respect of both applicants and further breach of the first applicant's Article 13 rights (read with Article 8), because the decision to remove O.D was made without proper risk assessment of O.D's injuries.

Key points:

- Care proceedings.
- Family life.
- Alleged physical assault.
- Removal of child.

---

[121] Exchange rate €1.3863 to £1.

Award: €15,000 (£12,415)[122] in total.

Welfare Benefits

England and Wales

R (BCD) v Birmingham Children's Trust [2023] EWHC 137 (Admin), 26 January 2023

Summary: The claimant was a British national child looked after by his Jamaican grandmother, who was unable to access welfare benefits as she had No Recourse to Public Funds ("**NRPF**") in the UK. The inability to access welfare benefits adversely impacted the claimant's family life and amounted to a violation of Article 8 and 14. Following judgment, the claim was settled at £10,000.

Key points:

- Welfare Benefits.
- Family life.
- Article 14.
- Indirect discrimination.
- Settlement.

Award: £10,000.

ECtHR

Grant v United Kingdom (2007) 44 E.H.R.R. 1, 23 August 2006

Summary: The applicant was born male and following gender reassignment surgery, she lived as a woman from 1963. Her application to receive her state pension at the age of 60 was refused and the age of 65 was applied to her, the age applicable for men. The applicant alleged that

[122] Exchange rate €1.2082 to £1.

this amounted to a breach of her rights under Article 8 of the ECHR, Article 1 of Protocol 1 and Article 14. The ECtHR held that there had been a violation of the applicant's Article 8 rights and acknowledged that there is now no justification for not legally recognising the legal change of gender, but that redress lay in the implementation of measures by the government to ensure compliance with Article 8.

Key points:

- Gender recognition.
- Private life.
- State pension payments.

Award: None.

Healthcare

England and Wales

Winspear v City Hospitals Sunderland NHS Foundation Trust [2015] EWHC 3250 (QB), 13 November 2015

Summary: Unbeknownst to the claimant, a "Do Not Attempt Cardio-Pulmonary Resuscitation" ("DNACPR") notice was placed on her son, who had severe disabilities, without her consent, when he was hospitalised with a chest infection. The court held that there had been a breach of Article 8 and when considering damages determined that a declaration was sufficient for just satisfaction on the basis that (i) the decision was made by the doctor prior to the publication of a judgment clarifying the law in such circumstances (ii) the doctor made the decision in good faith (iii) there was always a plan to consult the claimant about the decision (iv) the DNACPR notice was only in place for nine-ten hours and (v) the notice had no impact on her son's treatment or his death.

Key points:

- Medical treatment.
- Family and private life.
- Lack of consent.
- Duties to people with disabilities.

Award: None.

ECtHR

Glass v United Kingdom (2004) 39 E.H.R.R. 15, 9 March 2004

Summary: The applicants were a mother and son. The son had severe mental and physical disabilities. During the course of his repeated hospitalisations for life threatening deteriorations in his health, there were disagreements between the family and the doctors. The ECtHR held that the decisions to administer diamorphine to the son, and to place a "do not resuscitate" notice in his notes without the mother's knowledge amounted to a violation of Article 8. The ECtHR took into account, without reference to any other authorities, the anxiety, frustration and feeling of powerlessness felt by the mother.

Key points:

- Medical treatment.
- Private life.
- Duties to people with disabilities.
- Disagreements between family members and doctors.

Award: €10,000 (£6,716)[123].

M.A.K and R.K v United Kingdom (2010) 51 E.H.R.R. 14, 23 June 2010

Summary: The first applicant was the father of the second applicant. During the second applicant's admission to hospital for marks on her

123 Exchange rate €1.489 to £1.

legs, the doctor took tests and photographs of the second applicant without parental consent. The doctor also suggested that the second applicant had been abused and social services were contacted which impacted the first applicant's access to his daughter. It was ultimately held that there was insufficient evidence to suggest abuse; the marks were caused by a rare skin condition. The delay in seeking the opinion of an expert dermatologist was problematic. The damages awards took into account previous similar awards and the public humiliation felt by the first applicant.

Key points:

- Medical Treatment.
- Lack of consent.
- Family and private life.
- Reputation.

Award: €2,000 (£1,655)[124] to the first applicant and €4,500 (£3,725)[125] to the second applicant.

McDonald v United Kingdom (2015) 60 E.H.R.R. 1, 20 August 2014

Summary: The applicant required support following severe damage to her health as a result of a stroke and several falls. In particular, the applicant could not access a toilet or commode at night unaided and she applied for funding for a care package. The local authority accepted that the applicant had incontinence needs but reduced her care package requiring the applicant to use pads as opposed to providing support for her toileting needs, despite an assessment being delayed by a year. The period of approximately one years' delay in assessment breached the applicant's Article 8 rights, but the reduction in care provision was justified after an appropriate review. The award took into account the

124 Exchange rate €1.2082 to £1.

125 Exchange rate €1.2082 to £1.

support the applicant had received from carers and her partner to assist her with her nighttime toiletry needs.

Key points:

- Social care funding.
- Private life.
- Delay.
- Duties to people with disabilities.

Award: €1,000 (£797)[126].

Criminal Justice

England and Wales

Crook v Chief Constable of Essex Police [2015] EWHC 988 (QB), 2 March 2015

Summary: The police published an old photograph of the claimant on a wanted list stating that he was wanted for an alleged rape and his last known address. The court held that the release was a breach of his Article 8 rights, a breach of confidence and a breach of the Data Protection Act. The claimant was awarded substantial damages as he claimed under various heads of loss for (i) £57,750 special damages (ii) £5,000 general damages for personal injury (iii) £2,000 for basic damages for distress and the effects of disclosure and (iv) £3,000 for aggravated damages. The court did not delineate the proportion of the basic damages attributed to the human rights claim.

Key points:

- Police Disclosure.
- Private life.

126 Exchange rate €1.2542 to £1.

- Reputation.
- Damages for other claims.

Award: £2,000 (not solely for a breach of Article 8).

AB v Chief Constable of British Transport Police [2022] EWHC 2749 (KB), 7 November 2022

Summary: The claimant, who had Autistic Spectrum Disorder and severe anxiety, had a coping mechanism where he rubbed fabric between his fingers. He was reported to the police by two women alleging that he had touched them inappropriately. No charges were brought against the claimant. Nevertheless, the police retained the record of the complaints. The retention of the complaints amounted to a breach of the claimant's Article 8 rights. The first instance judge had awarded damages based on the Judicial College Guidelines and based on the distress actually caused to the claimant by the retention of his records. The claimant also received £15,000 in pecuniary damages and £6,000 in aggravated damages for the failure to undertake reviews in line with the police's data management policies.

Key points:

- Data retention.
- Police records.
- Private life.

Award: £15,000.

Northern Ireland

In the matter of an application by JR123 for Judicial Review [2022] NIQB 42, 9 June 2022

Summary: The inability of the applicant to have a conviction, from 1980, deemed as spent, resulted in the declaration of incompatibility but damages did not need to be awarded. The declaration of the court was sufficient to afford just satisfaction.

Key points:

- Data retention.
- Private life.
- Criminal records.

Award: None.

ECtHR

Keegan v United Kingdom (2007) 44 E.H.R.R. 33, 18 October 2006

Summary: Police officers forced entry into the applicant's home on the misunderstanding that one of the tenants was a person whom they suspected of robbery. The ECtHR held that basic steps were not carried out by police to verify the connection between the address and the offence under investigation. The forced entry, which caused the applicants considerable fear and alarm, could not be regarded as proportionate and amounted to a violation of Article 8. The award for non-pecuniary damages took into account the violent and shocking nature of the police entry into their property, the distress caused to the applicants and the medical reports that had been provided which indicated that the applicants would benefit from therapeutic intervention.

Key points:

- Forced entry by police.
- Private life.
- Psychological impact of police interaction.
- Parallel Article 13 claim.

Award: €3,000 (£2,018) to the parents and one child and €2,000 (£1,345) to the remaining three children.[127]

S and Marper v United Kingdom (2009) 48 E.H.R.R. 50, 4 December 2008

Summary: The applicants' fingerprints and cellular samples and DNA profiles has been retained by the authorities after the criminal proceedings against them had ended with an acquittal or had been discontinued. The ECtHR held that there had been a breach of Article 8, but the finding of a violation was sufficient just satisfaction.

Key points:

- Retention of biological data.
- Private life.
- Criminal record/ criminal proceedings.

Award: None.

Gillan and Quinton v United Kingdom (2010) 50 E.H.R.R. 45, 28 June 2010

Summary: Both applicants were stopped and searched by police near an arms fair. The first applicant was on his way to a demonstration nearby and the second applicant was a journalist who intended to film the protests. The ECtHR held that the use of the stop and search powers breached Article 8 (it therefore considered it unnecessary to determine claims made pursuant to Articles 5, 10 or 11). A violation was sufficient to afford just satisfaction, but the ECtHR agreed with the Government, who had submitted that the short duration of the stop and search meant that there was no call for monetary compensation.

---

127 Exchange rate €1.4869 to £1.

Key points:

- Protest rights.
- Private life.
- Stop and search powers.

Award: None.

MM v United Kingdom (App. No 24029/07), 29 April 2013.

Summary: The police retained details of a caution the applicant received. It was disclosed as part of a criminal record check, which led to the withdrawal of an offer of employment. The ECtHR was not satisfied that there were sufficient safeguards in place to prevent the disclosure of information that would violate the applicant's Article 8 rights and the interference was not in accordance with the law. The applicant did not make an application for non-pecuniary damages and the ECtHR held, as a result, there was no need to make such an award.

Key points:

- Data retention.
- Private life.
- Disclosure to third parties.
- No request for damages.

Award: None.

Catt v United Kingdom (2019) 69 E.H.R.R. 7, 24 January 2019

Summary: The retention of records confirming the applicant's involvement in protests organised by an organisation whose protests usually involved serious disorder and criminality, but where the applicant had not been implicated in such, was disproportionate. The applicant did not seek an award for non-pecuniary damages and one was not awarded.

Key Points:

- Criminal Records.
- Private life.
- Retention.
- Blanket policy.
- Sufficiency of safeguards.

Award: None.

Beghal v United Kingdom (2019) 69 E.H.R.R. 28, 28 May 2019

Summary: The applicant had been stopped, searched and questioned by the UK Border Force before her lawyer arrived when she returned from France, where her husband was incarcerated for terrorism offences. She was later charged with wilfully failing to comply. The regime allowed for detention of a person for up to nine hours, without reasonable suspicion. The ECtHR held that the powers were not sufficiently circumscribed and not subject to adequate safeguards against abuse.

Key Points:

- Terrorism.
- Private life.
- Stop and Search powers.

Award: None.

Gaughran v United Kingdom (Application no. 45245/15), 13 June 2020

Summary: The indefinite retention of the applicant's DNA profile, fingerprints and photograph when he had been convicted of driving with excess alcohol, without the possibility of review or other safeguards, was disproportionate. Although the applicant asked for non-pecuniary damages, he did not specify an amount.

Key Points:

- Criminal Records.
- Private life.
- Retention.
- Blanket policy.

Award: None.

DS v United Kingdom (Application no. 70988/12), 30 June 2021

Summary: The applicant received a sentence of six-months' conditional discharge for property damage, which the applicant was told would be deleted from her record after six months. Twenty years later, when she applied for an enhanced criminal record certificate, her previous convictions were disclosed. The mandatory disclosure requirements, from a regime in effect prior to 29 May 2013, of criminal record information in an enhanced criminal record certificate violated Article 8. The court concluded that there was no evidence that the risk of disclosure under the new regime caused the applicant any loss of opportunity in the social care or voluntary sector.

Key Points:

- Criminal Records.
- Private life.
- Disclosure.
- Blanket policy.

Award: None.

Prisons

England and Wales

Khosa v Secretary of State for Justice [2017] EWHC 1355 (Admin), 11 May 2017

Summary: The claimant was a prisoner serving a life sentence for murder. He complained about a decision by Secretary of State to make him subject to a child protection order that would prevent him from receiving visits from anyone under the age of 18. The defendant conceded that the order was not properly made in accordance with the claimant's Article 8 rights. On that basis, the court granted a declaration but not damages.

Key points:

- Prison restrictions.
- Private life.
- Defendant conceded violation.

Award: None.

R (Syed) v Secretary of State for Justice [2017] EWHC 727 (Admin), 7 April 2017

Summary: The claimant was a prisoner serving a life sentence. He claimed, inter alia, that restrictions on his ability to associate with other prisoners amounted to a breach of his rights under Article 8. The court held that the restrictions placed upon him went beyond what was acceptable in lawful detention and found that his rights had been breached. The breach arose out of a procedural error which would be remedied by a renewed transfer decision process and that, although the claimant claimed to have felt depressed and hopeless, the court had not received any medical evidence of any severe or permanent injury. The court determined that a finding of a violation was sufficient just satisfaction and therefore no award or declaration were made.

Key points:

- Prisoner restrictions.
- Private life.
- Procedural requirements.

Award: None.

<u>Scotland</u>

Greens, Petitioner [2011] CSOH 79, 12 May 2011

Summary: Where there was no integrated sanitation system in a prison and prisoners only had access to a chemical toilet, the requirement on prisoners to empty their own chemical toilets in front of others, until a sanitation team had been established, amounted to an infringement of their Article 8 rights.

Key points:

- Prison conditions.
- Private life.
- Article 8 as an alternative to Article 3.

Award: £500 to each claimant.

Shahid v Scottish Ministers [2015] UKSC 58, 14 October 2015

Summary: The claimant had been segregated from the prison population for 56 days. The failure to ensure the claimant's segregation was properly authorised and reviewed timeously rendered the segregation not in accordance with the law and disproportionate. Just satisfaction did not require an award of damages because (i) the claimant did not suffer any severe or permanent injury to his health; (ii) the degree of interference was relatively limited, given the attitude of the other prisoners towards him; and (iii) he was not isolated from all contact with other prisoners, was entitled to exercise and remained entitled to receive visits and to make telephone calls.

Key points:

- Prison conditions.
- Segregation.
- Private life.
- Article 8 as an alternative to Article 3.

Award: None.

Beggs v Scottish Ministers [2016] CSOH 80, 15 June 2016

Summary: The failure to deliver the claimant his correspondence, unopened, which would appear to have been privileged, whilst he was imprisoned amounted to an interference with his Article 8 rights. No award was made because there was no indication that the authorities read the petitioners mail, apologies were made, the respondent had undertaken an investigation, the system for recognition of privileged mail was altered following the petitioner's complaints, and there was no evidence of distress.

Key points:

- Prison and legal correspondence.
- Private life.
- System change.

Award: None.

McDowall v G4S Care and Justice Services (UK) Limited 2016 S.L.T. (Sh Ct) 371, 6 October 2016

Summary: Although the claim was unsuccessful, the court opined that the double handcuffing of a prisoner when escorted to hospital appointments would have resulted in a modest award had there been a finding that the conduct violated a person's Article 8 rights.

Key points:

- Prisoner treatment.
- Private life.
- Article 8 as an alternative to Article 3.

Award: None, but had there been a violation found the court would have awarded £100.

<u>ECtHR</u>

Boyle and Rice v United Kingdom (1988) 10 E.H.R.R. 425, 27 April 1988

Summary: The court found that stopping Mr Boyle's letters to a playwright friend was a breach of his rights under Article 8. The applicants did not seek damages, nevertheless, the court made an assessment on an equitable basis and granted an award to Mr Boyle only.

Key points:

- Prison correspondence.
- Private life.
- No request for damages.

Award: £3,000.

Campbell v United Kingdom (1993) 15 E.H.R.R. 137, 25 March 1992

Summary: The applicant was a serving prisoner. He complained that his correspondence with his solicitor and with the Commission was opened and read by the prison authorities. The ECtHR held that there was a breach of Article 8. The finding of a violation amounted to sufficient just satisfaction.

Key points:

- Prison and legal correspondence.
- Private life.

Award: None.

Faulkner v United Kingdom (2002) 35 E.H.R.R. 27, 4 September 2002

Summary: The applicant was a serving prisoner and brought a claim alleging a violation of his rights under Article 8 following the interference with his correspondence to a Scottish Minister of State. The ECtHR held that there was a breach of Article 8 but considered that although there will have been some frustration felt by the applicant, it was not of an intensity that would justify an award compensation.

Key points:

- Prison and legal correspondence.
- Private life.

Award: None.

Wainwright v United Kingdom (2007) 44 E.H.R.R. 40, 26 September 2006

Summary: The applicants were a mother and her son, who had cerebral palsy and severe arrested social and intellectual development. The applicants were visiting a family member in prison when they were strip-searched on suspicion that they were carrying drugs. The strip-searches were invasive and they were only provided with consent forms after the fact. The ECtHR held that there had been a breach of Article 8 (and Article 13) but no breach of Article 3. The applicants alleged they had not recovered from the psychological impact of the searches from which they had not fully recovered. The court took into account (without listing them or specifying which cases) previous cases in which awards were made for strip-searches, following which the court granted an award in line with previous awards.

Key points:

- Strip searches.
- Private life.
- Duties to people with disabilities.
- Parallel Article 13 claim.

Award: €3,000 (£2,026) to each applicant.[128]

Szuluk v United Kingdom (App. No. 36936/05), 2 September 2009

Summary: The applicant claimed that whilst he was a serving prisoner, his medical correspondence was monitored and that this amounted to a breach of his Article 8 rights. The ECtHR held that although such monitoring was limited to the prison medical officer viewing the applicant's medical correspondence to external professionals, the interference did not strike a fair balance with his Article 8 rights and amounted to a violation. The ECtHR considered that the circumstances of this case were such that the finding of a violation alone was insufficient to afford just satisfaction and instead made an award on an equitable basis.

128 Exchange rate €1.4811 to £1.

Key points:

- Prison correspondence.
- Private life.
- Private medical information.

Award: €1,000 (£892)[129].

Surveillance

ECtHR

Halford v United Kingdom (1997) 24 E.H.R.R. 523, 25 June 1997

Summary: The applicant was the Assistant Chief Constable of Merseyside Police until she retired in 1992. She brought proceedings against her employer alleging sex discrimination. The applicant had had her telephone calls intercepted, and subject to other harassing behaviour, after she brought her discrimination claim. The employer's conduct was aimed at collecting and using information against the applicant in the discrimination proceedings. The lack of regulation regarding this kind of surveillance amounted to a serious infringement of the applicant's Article 8 rights.

Key points:

- Interception of communications.
- Private life.
- Interference with court proceedings.
- Parallel Article 13 claim.

Award: £10,000.

---

[129] Exchange rate €1.1212 to £1.

PG and JH v United Kingdom (2008) 46 E.H.R.R. 51, 25 December 2001

Summary: The applicants brought a claim for breach of their rights under Article 6, 8 and 13 of the ECHR in respect of: (i) covert recording of them in a flat and in a police station which was used against them at trial; (ii) information obtained by police about the use of a telephone; (iii) the failure to disclose part of a police report to the defence at trial; and (iv) the decision of the court to hear evidence from a police officer in the absence of the defence. The court held that the use of covert listening devices in the flat and in the police station amounted to a violation of Article 8. The court took into account the fact that the applicants' rights had been breached in multiple ways and they had no effective remedy under domestic law and their feelings of frustration would not be sufficiently compensated by the finding of a violation alone.

Key points:

- Private life.
- Covert recording.
- Criminal prosecution.
- Parallel Article 13 claim.

Award: £1,000 each.

Taylor-Sabori v United Kingdom (2003) 36 E.H.R.R. 17, 22 January 2003

Summary: The interception of the applicant's pager messages by police and the use of them at his criminal trial amounted to a breach of his rights under Article 8 and Article 13. The ECtHR held that a finding of a violation was sufficient for just satisfaction.

Key points:

- Interception of communications.
- Private life.

- Absence of procedural safeguards.
- Parallel Article 13 claim.

Award: None.

Chalkley v United Kingdom (2003) 37 E.H.R.R. 30, 12 September 2003

Summary: The lack of a statutory system in place to regulate the use of surveillance devices planted by the police in the applicant's home amounted to a violation of Article 8. A finding of a violation was sufficient just satisfaction.

Key points:

- Regulation of surveillance devices.
- Private life.
- Not in accordance with the law.

Award: None.

Perry v United Kingdom (2004) 39 E.H.R.R. 3, 17 October 2003

Summary: The applicant's Article 8 rights were violated when he was covertly videotaped, for the purposes of identification, and the footage was used in the prosecution against him. The covert recording did not comply with the applicable codes of practice and was not in accordance with the law. The applicant had suffered feelings of frustration and an invasion of his privacy and therefore an award of non-pecuniary damage was to be made.

Key points:

- Covert recording.
- Private life.
- Not in accordance with the law.

Award: €1,500 (£1,046)[130].

Copland v United Kingdom (2007) 45 E.H.R.R. 37, 3 July 2006

Summary: The applicant was a personal assistant to the principal of a college, the college was a public body, and she discovered that the deputy principal at that college had directed that her telephone calls, emails and internet use be monitored. The ECtHR held that there was an absence of domestic law for regulating such monitoring and therefore the actions amounted to a violation of Article 8.

Key points:

- Surveillance of employees.
- Private life.

Award: €3,000 (£2,063)[131].

Liberty and Others v United Kingdom (2009) 48 E.H.R.R. 1, 1 October 2008

Summary: The applicant organisations brought a complaint that many of their telephone communications were intercepted by the government's Electronic Test Facility. A number of these telephone calls were between the organisations or were for giving legal advice to clients. The ECtHR held that the law in place at the time did not adequately establish safeguards to provide adequate protection against the abuse of power. It followed that there had been a violation of the applicants' Article 8 rights. The ECtHR determined that a finding of a violation was sufficient just satisfaction that negated the need for an award of non-pecuniary damages.

---

130 Exchange rate €1.4334 to £1.

131 Exchange rate €1.454 to £1.

Key points:

- Covert surveillance.
- Private life.
- Legal Advice.
- Sufficiency of safeguards.

Award: None.

RE v United Kingdom (2016) 63 E.H.R.R. 2, 27 October 2015

Summary: The applicant, a solicitor, was arrested and charged with several offences including inciting paramilitaries to murder and pervert the course of justice, based on covert recordings of the applicant in consultation with his clients at a police station. The police refused to give assurances to solicitors that their consultations would not be recorded. The relevant regime for covert surveillance did not have sufficient safeguards for the protection of material obtained by covert surveillance.

Key Points:

- Police Surveillance.
- Private life.
- Policies.
- Sufficiency of safeguards.

Award: €1,500 (£1,098)[132].

Big Brother Watch and others v United Kingdom (2022) 74 E.H.R.R. 17, 25 May 2021

Summary: The case concerned the bulk interception of cross-border communications under the Regulation of Investigatory Powers Act 2000. The failure to have in place adequate safeguards, such as an independent body to review the proportionality of the measures before and after

132 Exchange Rate €1.3657 to £1.

implementation violated Articles 8 and 10. There was no claim for non-pecuniary damages.

Key points:

- Bulk interception.
- Private life.
- Security services.
- Sufficiency of safeguards.
- No request for damages.
- Parallel Article 10 claim.

Award: None.

Privacy and Use of Private Information

England and Wales

W v Westminster City Council [2005] EWHC 102 (QB), 10 February 2005

Summary: The claimant brought a claim for libel and breach of Article 8 against the local authority and social workers, who produced a report for a child protection conference in which it was suggested that there were concerns that the claimant could be a predatory paedophile. This report was seen by the limited number of individuals in the conference.

This disclosure at the conference was an infringement of the claimant's Article 8 rights. In this case, the local authority had acted reasonably promptly when they were made aware of the breach, and the court awarded no damages. However, if the court indicated that, had it considered making an award, it would have awarded the claimant £1,000 on the basis that he had suffered genuine frustration and distress but not to the extent that medical intervention was required, nor had he been shunned by the people around him.

Key points:

- Disclosure to third parties.
- Private life.

Award: None, but had a violation been found £1,000 would have been awarded.

R (Kalluri) v Secretary of State for the Home Department [2015] EWHC 4073 (Admin), 15 December 2015

Summary: The Home Office's seizure and disposal of personal documents belonging to the claimants, such as a marriage certificate and education certificates, amounted to a breach of the claimants' Article 8 rights. The loss of important documents was distressing and inconvenient.

Key points:

- Data Destruction.
- Private life.

Award: £250.

ST (A Minor) and another v L Primary School [2020] EWHC 1046 (QB), 30 April 2020

Summary: The claimants, a child with Downs Syndrome ("ST") and her mother ("RF"), complained that the school breached of their Article 8 and Article 14 rights by sending a letter to all of the parents of children, in the same year as ST, referring to ST and her behaviour, without the consent of RF. The court held that this amounted to a breach of the claimants' rights under Article 8. In considering remedy, the court was keen to avoid "double recovery" for the various heads of claim, awarded ST £1,500 and RF £3,000 in respect of the data protection claims to acknowledge the distress they suffered, but did not consider it necessary for just satisfaction to award the claimants anything other than a declaration for the breach of their Article 8 and 14 rights specifically.

Key points:

- Disclosure to third parties.
- Private life.
- Duties to disabled people.
- Education.
- Parallel Article 14 claim.
- Damages for other claims.

Award: None.

<u>Northern Ireland</u>

King v Sunday Newspapers Ltd [2012] NICA 24, 29 June 2012

Summary: In this case, which considered the appropriate costs order, the judgment records the finding that the defendant infringed the appellant's family and private life by accusing him of involvement in serious criminal activity in newspaper articles. The impact was on the appellant and his family too.

Key points:

- Misuse of private information.
- Family and private life.
- Journalism.

Award: £1,000.

J20 v Facebook Ireland Ltd [2016] NIQB 98, 20 December 2016

Summary: References, in posts on social media, to the claimant being a "tout"/informer and to his children amounted to a misuse of private information. The defendant was found liable from the date that it had actual knowledge of the posts. In assessing an award of damages for misuse of private information, the court took into account that there was no finding of a link between any personal or psychiatric injury to the claimant as a result of the breaches and the limited nature, extent and duration of the breaches.

Key points:

- Misuse of private information.
- Private life.
- Social media.

Award: £3,000.

ECtHR

M.G v United Kingdom (2003) 36 E.H.R.R. 3, 24 December 2002

Summary: The applicant requested disclosure of his social services records relating to his time spent in care as a child. The refusal to permit access to his own records amounted to a breach of Article 8. In deciding on damages, the ECtHR considered that the applicant will have suffered some emotional distress and anxiety.

Key points:

- Access to personal data.
- Private life.

Award: €4,000 (£2,570)[133].

Peck v United Kingdom (2003) 36 E.H.R.R. 41, 28 April 2003

Summary: The local authority disclosed to the media CCTV, showing the applicant in the street with a knife attempting suicide, and then being

133 Exchange rate €1.5566 to £1.

disarmed and taken to a police station, amounted to a disproportionate and unjustified interference with his private life.

Key points:

- Disclosure of suicidal images.
- Private life.

Award: €11,800 (£8,135)[134].

Article 8 and Article 10 and Misuse of Private Information

England and Wales

Campbell v Mirror Group Newspaper [2004] UKHL 22, 6 May 2004

Summary: The claimant sued MGN Ltd for the articles that it published disclosing her drug addiction and details of the help she was seeking to tackle it, including taking covert photographs of her coming out of meetings. The House of Lords held that there had been a breach of the claimant's Article 8 rights which outweighed the defendant's Article 10 rights. The court restored the damages award made by Morland J in the first instance decision (Campbell v Mirror Group Newspapers [2002] EWHC 499(QB)): £2,500 for the distress and injury to feelings caused by the unjustified publication of the information and £1,000 in aggravated damages in light of the defendant's behaviour and attitude following the issue of the claimant's claim.

Key points:

- Misuse of private information.
- Private life.
- Newspaper journalism.
- Images.

---

[134] Exchange rate €1.4505 to £1.

- Damages for common law claim.

Award: £2,500.

McKennitt v Ash [2005] EWHC 3003 (QB), 21 December 2005

Summary: The claimant was a famous musician who brought an action against the defendant who sought to publish a book about her which she claimed contained private information. Two of the claimant's companies were also listed as claimants in this case. The court upheld a number of the claimant's complaints for breach of confidence e.g. where the information was of a particularly personal nature but did not uphold the complaints with regards to more anodyne information. The court awarded an injunction and damages for hurt feelings and distress.

Key points:

- Misuse of private information.
- Private life.
- Book publication.
- Information of a personal nature.
- Parallel common law claim.

Award: £5,000 for Ms McKennitt and a nominal award to her company.

Mosley v News Group Newspapers Ltd [2008] EWHC 1777 (QB), 24 July 2008

Summary: The claimant brought a claim against News Group Newspapers Ltd for breach of confidence and/or the unauthorised disclosure of personal information, said to infringe his rights of privacy after the defendant published an article about his attendance at an alleged Nazi themed sadomasochistic sex party. The article included photographs which were also available on the defendant's website along with videos from the event taken on a hidden camera supplied by the defendant. The court held that the claimant's Article 8 rights outweighed the defendant's Article 10 rights. The court found it necessary to afford a financial remedy that was sufficient to acknowledge the infringement of the claimant's rights and compensate him for the injury to feelings, the embarrassment and distress caused. The court accepted that his life was ruined by the story.

Key points:

- Misuse of private information.
- Private life.
- Newspaper journalism.
- Images.
- Parallel common law claim.

Award: £60,000.

Cooper v Turrell [2011] EWHC 3269 (QB), 12 December 2011

Summary: A disgruntled employee, Turrell, secretly recorded discussions with the director, and then started an internet campaign alleging that the claimant and the company were dishonest and had engaged in criminal conduct. There were claims for libel, breach of confidence and misuse of private information.

Key points:

- Misuse of private information
- Private life.
- Damages for common law claims.

Award: £30,000 but if the award had been for misuse of private information alone the award would have been £40,000.

AAA v Associated Newspapers Ltd [2012] EWHC 2103 (QB),[135] 25 July 2012

Summary: The claimant, a child, brought a claim for breach of privacy against the defendant arising out of the behaviour of its journalists such that her family life was infringed including the publication of her photograph and articles written about her. Although it was in the public interest for the article to be published about the existence of an MP's child as a result of an extramarital affair, there was no exceptional public interest to publish the image of a child without parental consent.

Key points:

- Rights of the child.
- Private life.
- Newspaper journalism.
- Images.

Award: £15,000.

Weller and others v Association Newspapers Limited [2014] EWHC 1163 (QB), 16 April 2014

Summary: The claimants, which included Mr Weller's young children, brought claims against the defendant newspaper following publication of their photographs without consent. The court concluded that the claimants' Article 8 rights outweighed the Article 10 rights of the defendant because the photographs were of the children's faces depicting a range of emotions. The court granted an award for each of the children on the basis of the following factors: (i) the misuse of private information related only to the facial features of the children (ii) the defendant did not know of the intrusive way in which the photographer obtained the photographs (iii) the article was withdrawn (iv) the actual readership of the Mail Online in the UK was only around 24,000 people, at the time,

[135] Decision not disturbed on appeal.

and (v) the young twin children would not have suffered any immediate embarrassment from the photographs unlike their older sister.

Key points:

- Misuse of private information.
- Private life.
- Rights of the child.
- Newspaper journalism.
- Images.

Award: £5,000 for the first claimant and £2,500 for the second and third claimant.

Ali and another v Channel 5 Broadcast Ltd [2018] EWHC 298 (Ch), 22 February 2018

Summary: The claimants were tenants in a residential property and their landlord sought repossession of the property which was filmed for a TV Show. This footage of the claimants was broadcast by the defendant's TV show. Although the TV show contributed to a debate of general public interest, the court found the information published went beyond that which was justified, noting that much of the show focused on the entertainment of the conflict between the claimants and the enforcement agents. The information was described as "fairly sensitive" and that the programme had a voyeuristic quality.

Summary:

- Misuse of private information.
- Private life.
- TV show.

Award: £10,000 per claimant.

ZXC v Bloomberg [2019] EWHC 970 (QB),[136] 17 April 2019

Summary: The claimant brought a claim for misuse of private information in relation to the publication on the defendant's website of information about him concerning a criminal investigation. The court held that the claimant did have a reasonable expectation of privacy and, on balance, the Article 10 rights of the defendant did not outweigh the claimant's Article 8 rights. In order to assess quantum, the court took into account the following factors: (i) the claimant was caused significant distress and anger by the publication that negatively impacted his dignity and standing (ii) there was no evidence of a wider impact on the claimant's lifestyle (iii) the information published was of a highly confidential nature (iv) the extent of the publication was limited and (v) the presentation of the information was serious and measured and therefore not sensationalist.

Key points:

- Misuse of private information.
- Private life.
- Criminal investigations.

Award: £25,000.

Bull v Desporte [2019] EWHC 1650 (QB), 26 June 2019

Summary: The claim concerned the publication of the defendant's book which included passages about the claimant's family, health and intimate relationship with the defendant, including a copyright claim relating to photographs contained in the book that were taken and sent by the claimant to the defendant. The court held that the claimant had a reasonable expectation of privacy in relation to the personal matters published in the book. The publication represented a serious infringement of his Article 8 rights, and those of his ex-wife and children. In order to assess the value of damages to be awarded, the court

[136] Decision not disturbed on appeal.

considered that (i) the publication of the book caused the claimant considerable distress including indirectly by virtue of the negative impact it had on his family and (ii) the nature of the information involved was '*at or towards the top end of the scale in terms of the protection to be afforded to it under Article 8*'.

Key points:

- Misuse of private information.
- Family and private life.
- Book publication.
- Images.

Award: £10,000.

Ali v Chief Constable of Bedfordshire Police [2023] EWHC 938 (KB), 25 April 2023

Summary: The claimant made a report to police about her ex-husband's suspected drug dealing. The claimant asked not to be identified as she feared repercussions from him. The police passed this information to the local borough council including the identification of the claimant. This information was passed to the ex-husband by the unlawful disclosure of a council employee. The claimant claimed that the information provided by police amounted to a breach of her GDPR rights, a misuse of private information, a breach of confidence and was incompatible with her rights under Article 8. The court held that the claimant's rights under these heads of claim had been breached and awarded £3,000 under the data protection regime. No separate award was required under the HRA but the court concluded that had it considered an Article 8 violation alone it would have awarded £3,000.

Key points:

- Police disclosure to local authorities.
- Relationship between GDPR and Article 8.
- Private life.

Award: £3,000, had it been necessary to make such an award.

ECtHR

Gaskin v United Kingdom (1990) 12 E.H.R.R. 36, 7 July 1989

Summary: The applicant was placed into care following the death of his mother less than a year after his birth. He broadly remained in care (save for short periods) until he reached 18 years old. The applicant sought disclosure of information about his time in care but the local authority declined to provide it. The applicant applied to the ECtHR and alleged that the continued refusal to disclose his records amounted to a breach of his rights under Article 8 and Article 10. The ECtHR held that there was a breach of the applicant's Article 8 rights (but no breach of Article 10). In reaching its decision on damages the ECtHR acknowledged the emotional distress and anxiety felt by the claimant.

Key points:

- Social care.
- Access to records.
- Private life.

Award: £5,000.

CHAPTER NINE

ARTICLE 9

1. Everyone has the right to freedom of thought, conscience and religion; this right includes freedom to change his religion or belief and freedom, either alone or in community with others and in public or private, to manifest his religion or belief, in worship, teaching, practice and observance.

2. Freedom to manifest one's religion or beliefs shall be subject only to such limitations as are prescribed by law and are necessary in a democratic society in the interests of public safety, for the protection of public order, health or morals, or for the protection of the rights and freedoms of others.

Introduction

1. An interference with the right to freedom of thought, conscience and/or religion is often compensated for by and/or within the framework of the Equality Act 2010. Findings of an Article 9 breach alone is rare in domestic case law and quantification of damages rarer still.

2. Consequently, the quantification of Article 9 breaches is best found in the Strasbourg case law. Even in the ECtHR, the instances of violations of Article 9 in respect of the UK (with one of the two cases appearing the Chapter on Article 12) or states of comparative GDP are limited in number and skewed by the associated violations found.

3. This chapter focusses on cases where the prominent violation concerns Article 9 with fewer associated breaches. Practitioners' attention is drawn to *Taganrog LRO and others v Russia* (Application

nos. 32401/10 and 19 others, 7 June 2022) includes an extensive appendix of different awards for violations of Article 9, read with Articles 5, 10, 11 and Article 1 of Protocol 1.

United Kingdom

Eweida v United Kingdom [2013] IRLR 231, 15 January 2013

Summary: The only successful case, of the four cases concerning the UK considered by the ECtHR, concerned the entitlement of Ms Eweida to wear a visible cross as a form of practice of her Christianity whilst working. The ECtHR concluded that the policy of not allowing her to wear her cross at work was disproportionate because her cross was discrete and there was no evidence that other previously authorised religious clothing by her employer impacted the employer's brand or image. Further, as the company subsequently amended its policy, the ECtHR concluded that there was no real encroachment on the rights of others. The ECtHR considered that Ms Eweida did not suffer a loss of earnings. The ECtHR awarded non-pecuniary damages in recognition of the anxiety, frustration and distress caused by the violation over five months.

Key Points:

- Manifest religion.
- Religious clothing at work.

Award: €2,000 (£1,667)[137].

[137] Exchange rate €1.2 to £1.

Other states

Kimlya and others v Russia (Application nos. 76836/01 and 32782/03), 1 March 2010

Summary: The authorities refused to register a Church of Scientology because of the requirement of fifteen years' presence in a given territory to obtain legal personality as a religious organisation. The ECtHR held that the refusal to register interferes with the right to religion and association which affects the group and individual members. The applicant was not denied registration because of a special feature of the religion but because of a presence issue. The prolonged period before registration was not justified and did not relate to any pressing social need.

Key Points:

- Registration.
- Presence requirement.
- Parallel Article 11 claim.

Award: €5,000 (£4,508)[138].

Korostelev v Russia (Application no. 29290/10), 12 August 2020

Summary: the imposition of a disciplinary punishment on a prisoner for praying at night, outside the prison regime, violated the applicant's Article 9 rights.

Key Points:

- Religious practice.
- Prison regime.

[138] Exchange rate €1.1092 to £1.

Award: €2,600 (£2,342)[139].

Centre of Societies for Krishna Consciousness in Russia and Frolov v Russia (Application no. 37477/11), 23 February 2022

Summary: The applicant complained that Russian authorities published a brochure called "Watch out for cults", which had given a hostile assessment of the applicant's institution calling it a "totalitarian cult", "destructive" and money-greedy, and accused the applicant of "psychological manipulation" and "zombification" of the youth. The court considered that the brochure went further than simply publishing the views of religious scholars which would have been acceptable in a democratic society. The use of derogatory language and making unsubstantiated allegations violated the applicant's rights.

Key Points:

- Commentary on religion.
- Parallel Article 11 claim.

Award: €7,500 (£6,285)[140].

Milshteyn v Russia (Application no. 1377/14), 31 January 2023

Summary: The complaint concerned the banning of the Elle-Ayat religious group as an extremist organisation based on a linguist's findings that an Elle-Ayat publication contained indications of extremist views including views inducing a refusal of medical assistance on religious grounds. The court found there was a violation of Article 9 read with Article 11, and of Article 10, as the courts had not undertaken its own analysis of the publications in question and considered that the

---

139 Exchange rate €1.11 to £1.

140 Exchange rate €1.1933 to £1.

publications were not indicative of coercion or undue pressure to refuse medical treatment.

Key Points:

- Religious views.
- Refusal of medical treatment.
- Parallel Article 10 and 11 claims.

Award: €9,750 (£8,589)[141].

Nabokikh and others v Russia (Application no. 19428/11 and 6 others), 31 January 2023

Summary: Jehovah's witnesses organised and/or participated in religious meetings and/or assemblies held on premises which were owned or rented for that purpose. Multiple meetings and/or assemblies were interrupted by police officers for differing reasons. The police ordered meetings to stop or stayed on premises to make recordings of meetings, checking attendee documents, and/or questioning attendees. The court considered the sanctions did not have a clear and foreseeable legal basis. The assemblies were peaceful in nature and disruption by the police did not pursue a pressing social need. The search warrants were overly broad which gave police unrestricted discretion and resulted in intrusive searches.

Key Points:

- Religious meetings.
- Police raids.

Award: Between €500 and €7,500 (£440 and £6,607) which reflected the awards sought, save that where awards were sought for over €7,500

[141] Exchange rate €1.1352 to £1.

(£6,607), in which case the award made was capped at €7,500 (£6,607).[142]

Ossewaarde v Russia (Application no. 27227/17), 7 June 2023

Summary: The applicant was fined for carrying out missionary work without having notified the authorities, by inviting people to his home for prayer and Bible reading. The fine was higher for non-nationals than it would have been for nationals. The court considered there was no evidence of the applicant using inappropriate methods of proselytism or coercion. The laws excluding private homes from the list of possible places to impart information on religion lacked justification by the state and left no room for people who were engaged in individual evangelism.

Key Points:

- Religious meetings.
- Legislation without necessity reasoned.
- Associated Article 14 violation.

Award: €10,000 (£8,584)[143].

---

[142] Exchange rate €1.1352 to £1.

[143] Exchange rate €1.165 to £1.

CHAPTER TEN

ARTICLE 10

1. Everyone has the right to freedom of expression. This right shall include freedom to hold opinions and to receive and impart information and ideas without interference by public authority and regardless of frontiers. This Article shall not prevent States from requiring the licensing of broadcasting, television or cinema enterprises.

2. The exercise of these freedoms, since it carries with it duties and responsibilities, may be subject to such formalities, conditions, restrictions or penalties as are prescribed by law and are necessary in a democratic society, in the interests of national security, territorial integrity or public safety, for the prevention of disorder or crime, for the protection of health or morals, for the protection of the reputation or rights of others, for preventing the disclosure of information received in confidence, or for maintaining the authority and impartiality of the judiciary.

Introduction

1. Article 10 protects the right to freedom of expression and is most often engaged in circumstances relating to protests and publications. However, as will be seen below, unless the violation of Article 10 is coupled with the violation of another Article, the finding of a violation of Article 10 is often considered sufficient just satisfaction.

2. The implication is, therefore, that to persuade a court that non-pecuniary damages are necessary to achieve just satisfaction, concrete evidence of harm and/or prejudice is essential.

3. Practitioners are invited to consider the chapter on Article 8 for parallel claims that involve Article 10 violations.

Journalism

England and Wales

R v Secretary of State for the Home Department ex parte Simms [2000] 2 AC 115, 8 July 1999

Summary: A blanket requirement that journalists sign an undertaking, to the effect that they would not use any information from oral interview with a prisoner in their professional capacity, amounted an unjustifiable curtailment of the claimant's right to freedom of expression. The Secretary of State's policy, as well as prison governors' administrative decisions made pursuant to the policy, was declared to be unlawful.

Key Points:

- Prisoners.
- Policy challenge.
- Pre-dates HRA.

Award: None.

ECtHR

Sunday Times v United Kingdom (1981) 3 E.H.R.R. 31, 6 November 1980

Summary: The Sunday Times began a series of articles intending to assist parents who had been affected by the consequences of the drug Thalidomide to negotiate generous settlement offers in their cases against the State. The Attorney-General obtained an injunction restraining the publication of one of the articles in the series. The Sunday Times claimed that the injunction was a breach of their Article 10 rights. The ECtHR held that The Sunday Times' Article 10 rights had been breached, as the interference had not been justified under Article 10(2). No award for non-pecuniary damage was made.

Key Points:

- Freedom of the press.
- Matters of public interest.
- No request for damages.

Award: None.

The Observer and The Guardian v United Kingdom (1992) 14 E.H.R.R. 153, 26 November 1991

Summary: The appellant newspaper companies complained following the granting of an interlocutory injunction, which prevented them from publishing extracts from a controversial book. They brought claims that the injunction breached their rights under Article 10, Article 13 and Article 14. Although the interference with the Article 10 rights of the publishers was prescribed by law and the measure was put in place for the legitimate aim of protecting national security and maintaining the authority of the judiciary, the ECtHR held that the objectives were insufficient to justify the continuation of the interference.

Key Points:

- Newspaper journalism.
- Article 13 and Article 14.
- No request for damages.

Award: None.

Tolstoy Miloslavsky v United Kingdom (1995) 20 E.H.R.R. 442, 13 July 1995

Summary: The applicant had unsuccessfully defended domestic libel proceedings and was ordered to pay £1,500,000 in damages. An injunction preventing further publication of a specific pamphlet was awarded. The applicant alleged (amongst other claims) that the damages award and the injunction amounted to a breach of his Article 10 rights. The ECtHR held that the size of the award, coupled with the lack of adequate and effective judicial safeguards against such a disproportionate award, was a violation of the applicant's Article 10 rights. Although, it did not find that the injunction was a violation of his rights.

Key Points:

- Damages in libel.
- Non-journalistic publications.
- No request for damages.

Award: None.

Goodwin v United Kingdom (1996) 22 E.H.R.R. 123, 27 March 1996

Summary: The claimant was a journalist who received information about a company's financial difficulties. The claimant contacted the company for comment ahead of publishing an article. The company was of the view that the source of the claimant's information was stolen documents and successfully obtained an interim injunction preventing the publication of the claimant's article and a High Court order requiring the claimant to disclose the identity of her source. The claimant refused to give up her source and was fined £5,000 for contempt of court. The ECtHR held that the claimant's Article 10 rights had been breached by the disclosure order and the fine imposed on her for contempt of court. The ECtHR unanimously agreed that a finding of a violation of the claimant's Article 10 rights was adequate just satisfaction for non-pecuniary damage.

Key Points:

- Journalistic sources.
- Balancing exercise.

Award: None.

Steel and Morris v United Kingdom (2005) 41 E.H.R.R. 22, 15 February 2005

Summary: Ms Steel and Mr Morris were members of a small group that campaigned on social and environmental issues, and they had been involved in the distribution of leaflets campaigning against a well-known fast-food chain. The chain sued Ms Steel and Mr Morris for libel. They represented themselves and lost. Damages were awarded against them; £36,000 from Ms Steel and £40,000 from Mr Morris (following an appeal in which the original damages awarded against them were reduced). They complained to the ECtHR that the refusal of legal aid was a breach of their rights under Article 6, and the case and its outcome was a disproportionate interference with their rights under Article 10. The ECtHR held that there had been a breach of Article 10 and Article 6 in this case. The court made an award of damages for non-pecuniary loss by way of just satisfaction in recognition of the fact that (i) Ms Steel and Mr Morris had to represent themselves in legal proceedings that were particularly difficult and lengthy and (ii) the result was that they both suffered anxiety and disruption to their lives much more so than a represented litigant would have.

Key Points:

- Inequality of arms in court proceedings.
- Parallel Article 6 claim.

Award: €20,000 (£13,794) awarded to Ms Steel. €15,000 (£10,346) awarded to Mr Morris.[144]

Financial Times Ltd v United Kingdom (2010) 50 E.H.R.R. 46, 15 December 2009

Summary: The applicants were ordered by a domestic court to disclose leaked documents that an anonymous source had provided them. The documents contained information about the planned takeover of a brewing company. The ECtHR held that the order, to disclose the documents, was a breach of the applicants' Article 10 rights. The applicants claimed for the reimbursement of their costs and expenses, but no specific claim was made for non-pecuniary damages. The ECtHR did not award non-pecuniary damages.

Key points:

- Disclosure order.
- Journalistic sources.

Award: None.

Pal v United Kingdom (Application no. 44261/19), 28 February 2022

Summary: The applicant was a journalist who was arrested for harassment of a subject of her article; a person with whom she previously had heated exchanges in the past. The applicant brought a claim that her arrest and detention breached her Article 10 rights. The ECtHR held that there was no evidence that the police carried out the requisite rights balancing exercise prior to her arrest. There had been a breach of her Article 10 rights. The applicant claimed €10,000 in non-pecuniary damages. In making a smaller award for non-pecuniary damage, the

---

[144] Exchange rate €1.4499 to £1.

ECtHR acknowledged the frustration and inconvenience that was caused as a result of her arrest and prosecution.

Key points:

- Arrest and detention.
- Journalism.
- Criminal prosecution.

Award: €2,500 (£2,095)[145].

Protest

England and Wales

R (Leigh and others) v Commissioner of Police of the Metropolis [2022] EWHC 527 (Admin), 11 March 2022

Summary: The claimants sought to hold a public vigil in London in memory of a woman who had been murdered in March 2021. The vigil was characterised by police as unlawful, on the basis that it contravened the restrictions on public gatherings in the Coronavirus Regulations that were in place at that time. This approach by the police had a deterrent effect on the organising of the vigil. The court held that the approach by the police amounted to a disproportionate interference with the claimants' Article 10 and Article 11 rights. The claimants claimed £7,500 in damages. The court held that the judgment, coupled with a declaration that the police's decisions were unlawful, was sufficient to afford the claimants just satisfaction.

Key Points:

- Parallel Article 11 claim.

---

145 Exchange rate €1.1933 to £1.

- Blanket prohibitions.

Award: None.

ECtHR

Bowman v United Kingdom (1998) 26 E.H.R.R. 1, 19 February 1988

Summary: The claimant was an anti-abortion campaigner, who was arrested after she distributed approximately 25,000 leaflets prior to the general election setting out the position of three candidates. She was prosecuted under section 75 of the Representation of the People Act 1983 for spending more than £5, as an unauthorised person, on publications with the aim of promoting or procuring the election of a candidate in the six weeks prior to the election. The ECtHR held that the £5 limit was a disproportionate response to the need to safeguard equality between parliamentary candidates and was therefore an unlawful interference with Article 10. The ECtHR determined that a finding of a violation of the claimant's rights was sufficient just satisfaction.

Key Points:

- Political campaigning.
- Arrest.

Award: None.

CHAPTER ELEVEN

ARTICLE 11

1. Everyone has the right to freedom of peaceful assembly and to freedom of association with others, including the right to form and to join trade unions for the protection of his interests.

2. No restrictions shall be placed on the exercise of these rights other than such as are prescribed by law and are necessary in a democratic society in the interests of national security or public safety, for the prevention of disorder or crime, for the protection of health or morals or for the protection of the rights and freedoms of others. This Article shall not prevent the imposition of lawful restrictions on the exercise of these rights by members of the armed forces, of the police or of the administration of the State.

Introduction

1. Whilst there are several domestic cases with a standalone finding that Article 11 has been violated, the remedy sought and/or granted has been a declaration (see for example *National Union of Professional Foster Carers v the Certification Officer* [2021] EWCA Civ 548 or *Secretary of State for Business and Trade v Mercer* [2024] UKSC 12).

2. Where the courts have found a violation of Article 11 with other Articles, the awards are dealt with in earlier chapters.

3. This chapter outlines the Strasbourg case law on freestanding Article 11 violations.

United Kingdom

Young v United Kingdom (1983) 5 E.H.R.R. 201, 18 October 1982

Summary: The three applicants, Mr Young, Webster and James, were dismissed from their jobs because they refused to join a trade union in line with the conditions of employment imposed by the employer. The condition of employment amounted to a violation of Article 11. Non-pecuniary damages were awarded to acknowledge the stress and anxiety experienced by the applicants, the financial problems they experienced, and the difficulties they encountered in obtaining other employment.

Key Points:

- Trade Union Membership.
- Employment.

Award: Mr. Young – £2,000; Mr. Webster – £3,000; and Mr. James – £6,000.

Wilson and Others v United Kingdom (2002) 35 E.H.R.R. 20, 2 October 2002

Summary: The legal framework in place at the time allowed for employers to cease to recognise trade unions and offer an inducement to employees to relinquish the right to union representation, which effectively undermined a trade union's ability to represent its members' interests. This amounted to a violation of Article 11. Non-pecuniary damages were awarded in recognition of the anger, frustration and emotional distress that resulted from the unsuccessful attempts to seek redress before the domestic courts.

Key Points:

- Trade Union Membership.

Award: €7,730 (£4,871) to each applicant.[146]

Other states

Maestri v Italy (2004) 39 E.H.R.R. 38, 17 February 2004

Summary: Disciplinary action was taken against the applicant, who was an acting president of a national court, for being a Freemason, on the basis that there was an incompatibility between the Masonic and judicial oaths. This violated Article 11 because the domestic law did not contain sufficient information to satisfy the condition of foreseeability, that a judge would know they should refrain from joining the Freemasons. Damages were awarded based on assumed psychological and mental suffering caused by the imposition and enforcement of disciplinary sanction.

Key Points:

- Impact of membership of third-party organisations on employment.

Award: €10,000 (£6,769)[147].

Adefdromil v France (Application no. 32191/09), 2 October 2014

Summary: The applicant was an association arguing that there was a violation of Article 11 arising from the prohibition on members of the military from joining trade unions and the prohibition on such associations taking legal action to defend collective professional interests. The court concluded that a blanket prohibition on professional associations for military personnel taking any legal action undermined the essence of the freedom afforded under Article 11, and that the state's

[146] Exchange rate €1.5868 to £1.

[147] Exchange rate €1.4774 to £1.

prohibition was disproportionate. Non-pecuniary damages were claimed on the basis that the group had been portrayed as a threat to military order.

Key Points:

- Trade Union Membership.

Award: €5,000 (£3,944)[148].

---

148 Exchange rate €1.2678 to £1.

CHAPTER TWELVE

ARTICLE 12

Men and women of marriageable age have the right to marry and to found a family, according to the national laws governing the exercise of this right.

Introduction

1. There are limited domestic cases involving damages for violations of Article 12 because:

    a. Routinely, the finding of a violation amounts to adequate just satisfaction in respect of violations of Article 12. It is only in exceptional circumstances where damages would be awarded for distress or humiliation arising from breaches of a person's Article 12 and 14 rights. These are where the distress is of exceptional gravity, and/or without medical or other cogent corroborative evidence (*R (Baiai) and others v Secretary of State for the Home Department* [2006] EWHC 1035 (Admin) at [34] and [36]).

    b. Similarly to Article 9, as marriage and civil partnerships are protected characteristics under the Equality Act 2010, discrimination claims may largely be caught by the enforcement provisions (and remedy framework) within that act.

2. The exceptional circumstances where damages are awarded is evident by the lack of domestic cases and (as at the date of drafting) there being only eleven Strasbourg judgments on merits and just satisfaction. In five of the eleven Strasbourg judgments, the finding

of a violation was considered sufficient; in four out of the eleven judgments, damages were awarded following the finding of violations of more than one Article (aside from Article 13 and 14).

United Kingdom

O'Donoghue and others v United Kingdom (2011) 53 E.H.R.R. 1, 14 March 2011

Summary: A scheme that required persons subject to immigration control to have entry clearance for the purpose of marriage or have a certificate of approval to marry in the United Kingdom, unless they were marrying in accordance with the rite of the Church of England, violated Articles 12, and 9 and 12 read with Article 14.

Key Points:

- Parallel Articles 9 and 14 claims.
- Immigration control.

Award: €8,500 (£7,374) to each applicant.[149]

Other states

Jaremowicz v Poland (Application no. 24023/03), 5 January 2010

Summary: The refusal of permission to a prisoner to marry was found to violate Article 12. The grounds for refusal were not linked to prison security or prevention of disorder and was limited to their assessment of the nature and the quality of the prisoner's relationship with his fiancé.

[149] Exchange rate €1.1527 to £1.

Key Points:

- Prisoner's right to marry.

Award: €1,000 (£883)[150].

Chernetskiy v Ukraine (Application no. 44316/07), 8 December 2016

Summary: The failure to finalise the applicant's divorce and provide him a divorce certificate in prison for three years and seven months, so that he could re-marry, amounted to an unjustified impairment to the applicant's right to marry.

Key Points:

- Administrative Delay.
- Prisoner's right to marry.

Award: €3,000 (£2,534)[151].

150 Exchange rate €1.1327 to £1.

151 Exchange rate €1.1838 to £1.

CONCLUSION

1. You may have come to the end of this book and thought, "where are Articles 13 and 14" or the rights contained in the First Protocol in Part II of Schedule 1 HRA.

2. The answer is easy on Article 13. Schedule 1 HRA does not include reference to Article 13.

3. Article 14 states that:

   "*enjoyment of the rights and freedoms set forth in the European Convention on Human Rights shall be secured without discrimination on any ground such as sex, race, colour, language, religion, political or other opinion, national or social origin, association with a national minority, property, birth or other status.*"

   Article 14 is dependent on a claim falling within the ambit of a particular Convention right, and cases which engage Article 14 are contained in the chapter concerning the operant Convention right.

4. As to the First Protocol referenced in Part II of Schedule 1 HRA: peaceful enjoyment of possessions most explicitly considers the rights in respect of property and therefore leaning more into the sphere of pecuniary damages; and education and free elections appeared, to the authors, to be the specific, quintessential rights where performance prevailed over non-pecuniary damages. Nevertheless, perhaps the addition of those Articles lies in this book's future.

MORE BOOKS BY LAW BRIEF PUBLISHING

A selection of our other titles available now:-

'A Practical Guide to Probation Breaches and Other Applications' by Mark Thomas
'A Practical Guide to Remarriage and Divorce' by Cordelia Williams & Claire Howard
'A Practical Guide to Privacy, Transparency, Reporting Restrictions and Closed Proceedings in the Court of Protection' by Laura Mannering
'Beaumont on Barristers – A Guide to Defending Disciplinary Proceedings (Second Edition)' by Marc Beaumont
'A Practical Guide to Payments for Environmental Services' by Ben Sharples
'A Practical Guide to the Law of Pregnancy and Maternity at Work' by Rebecca Thomas
'A Practical Guide to Redundancy – Second Edition' by Philip Hyland & Collette Moore
'A Practical Guide to International Issues for Scottish Family Lawyers' by Susie Mountain, Donna McKay, Ken MacDonald
'A Practical Guide to the Law on Deprivation of Liberty' by Ben Troke
'A Practical Guide to Rights over Airspace and Subsoil – Second Edition' by Daniel Gatty
'A Practical Guide to the Law in Relation to Inquests' by Ramya Nagesh
'A Practical Guide to the Construction and Rectification of Wills and Trust Instruments (Second Edition)' by Edward Hewitt
'A Practical Guide to Data Protection in Social Housing' by Clare Paterson
'A Practical Guide to Spousal Maintenance – Second Edition' by Liz Cowell
'A Practical Guide to International Parental Child Abduction Law (England and Wales)' by Dr Onyója Momoh
'A Practical Guide to Deprivation of British Citizenship' by Sean Ell
'A Practical Guide to Commercial Property Service Charges' by Rachel Garton
'A Practical Guide to Clinical Negligence – Third Edition' by Geoffrey Simpson-Scott (Geoff)
'A Practical Guide to the Rights of Grandparents in Children Proceedings – Second Edition' by Stuart Barlow

'The Electronic Communications Code: A Practical Guide – Second Edition' by Kerry Bretherton KC, James Castle, Mark Loveday
'A Practical Guide to the Independent School Standards – September 2023 Edition' by Sarah McKimm
'A Practical Guide to Estate Administration and Crypto Assets' by Richard Marshall
'A Practical Guide to Parental Alienation in Private and Public Law Children Cases' by Sam King QC & Frankie Shama
'Contested Heritage – Removing Art from Land and Historic Buildings' by Richard Harwood QC, Catherine Dobson, David Sawtell
'The Limits of Separate Legal Personality: When Those Running a Company Can Be Held Personally Liable for Losses Caused to Third Parties Outside of the Company' by Dr Mike Wilkinson
'A Practical Guide to Transgender Law' by Robin Moira White & Nicola Newbegin
'A Practical Guide to 'Stranded Spouses' in Family Law' by Mani Singh Basi
'A Practical Guide to Residential Freehold Conveyancing' by Lorraine Richardson
'A Practical Guide to Pensions on Divorce for Lawyers' by Bryan Scant
'A Practical Guide to Challenging Sham Marriage Allegations in Immigration Law' by Priya Solanki
'A Practical Guide to Digital Communications Evidence in Criminal Law' by Sam Willis
'A Practical Guide to Legal Rights in Scotland' by Sarah-Jane Macdonald
'A Practical Guide to New Build Conveyancing' by Paul Sams & Rebecca East
'A Practical Guide to Inherited Wealth on Divorce' by Hayley Trim
'A Practical Guide to Practice Direction 12J and Domestic Abuse in Private Law Children Proceedings' by Rebecca Cross & Malvika Jaganmohan
'A Practical Guide to Confiscation and Restraint' by Narita Bahra QC, John Carl Townsend, David Winch
'A Practical Guide to the Law of Forests in Scotland' by Philip Buchan
'A Practical Guide to Health and Medical Cases in Immigration Law' by Rebecca Chapman & Miranda Butler
'A Practical Guide to Bad Character Evidence for Criminal Practitioners by Aparna Rao
'A Practical Guide to Extradition Law post-Brexit' by Myles Grandison et al
'A Practical Guide to Hoarding and Mental Health for Housing Lawyers' by Rachel Coyle

'Stephens on Contractual Indemnities' by Richard Stephens
'A Practical Guide to the EU Succession Regulation' by Richard Frimston
'A Practical Guide to Solicitor and Client Costs – Second Edition' by Robin Dunne
'Constructive Dismissal – Practice Pointers and Principles' by Benjimin Burgher
'A Practical Guide to Religion and Belief Discrimination Claims in the Workplace' by Kashif Ali
'A Practical Guide to the Law of Medical Treatment Decisions' by Ben Troke
'Fundamental Dishonesty and QOCS in Personal Injury Proceedings: Law and Practice' by Jake Rowley
'A Practical Guide to the Law in Relation to School Exclusions' by Charlotte Hadfield & Alice de Coverley
'A Practical Guide to Divorce for the Silver Separators' by Karin Walker
'The Right to be Forgotten – The Law and Practical Issues' by Melissa Stock
'A Practical Guide to Planning Law and Rights of Way in National Parks, the Broads and AONBs' by James Maurici QC, James Neill et al
'A Practical Guide to Election Law' by Tom Tabori
'A Practical Guide to the Law in Relation to Surrogacy' by Andrew Powell
'A Practical Guide to Claims Arising from Fatal Accidents – Second Edition' by James Patience
'A Practical Guide to Asbestos Claims' by Jonathan Owen & Gareth McAloon
'A Practical Guide to Stamp Duty Land Tax in England and Northern Ireland' by Suzanne O'Hara
'A Practical Guide to the Law of Farming Partnerships' by Philip Whitcomb
'A Practical Guide to the Law of Unlawful Eviction and Harassment – Second Edition' by Stephanie Lovegrove
'A Practical Guide to Costs in Personal Injury Claims – Second Edition' by Matthew Hoe
'A Practical Guide to the General Data Protection Regulation (GDPR) – Second Edition' by Keith Markham
'A Practical Guide to Working with Litigants in Person and McKenzie Friends in Family Cases' by Stuart Barlow
'Protecting Unregistered Brands: A Practical Guide to the Law of Passing Off' by Lorna Brazell
'A Practical Guide to Secondary Liability and Joint Enterprise Post-Jogee' by Joanne Cecil & James Mehigan

'A Practical Guide to the Pre-Action RTA Claims Protocol for Personal Injury Lawyers' by Antonia Ford
'A Practical Guide to Neighbour Disputes and the Law' by Alexander Walsh
'A Practical Guide to Coercive Control for Legal Practitioners and Victims' by Rachel Horman
'A Practical Guide to the Law of Driverless Cars – Second Edition'
by Alex Glassbrook, Emma Northey & Scarlett Milligan
'A Practical Guide to TOLATA Claims' by Greg Williams
'A Practical Guide to Elderly Law – Second Edition' by Justin Patten
'A Practical Guide to Responding to Housing Disrepair and Unfitness Claims' by Iain Wightwick
'A Practical Guide to the Law of Bullying and Harassment in the Workplace' by Philip Hyland
'How to Be a Freelance Solicitor: A Practical Guide to the SRA-Regulated Freelance Solicitor Model' by Paul Bennett
'A Practical Guide to Prison Injury Claims' by Malcolm Johnson
'A Practical Guide to Advising Clients at the Police Station' by Colin Stephen McKeown-Beaumont
'A Practical Guide to Antisocial Behaviour Injunctions – Second Edition' by Iain Wightwick
'Practical Mediation: A Guide for Mediators, Advocates, Advisers, Lawyers, and Students in Civil, Commercial, Business, Property, Workplace, and Employment Cases' by Jonathan Dingle with John Sephton
'The Mini-Pupillage Workbook' by David Boyle
'A Practical Guide to Crofting Law' by Brian Inkster
'A Practical Guide to the Law of Domain Names and Cybersquatting' by Andrew Clemson
'A Practical Guide to the Law of Gender Pay Gap Reporting' by Harini Iyengar
'NHS Whistleblowing and the Law' by Joseph England
'Employment Law and the Gig Economy' by Nigel Mackay & Annie Powell
'A Practical Guide to Noise Induced Hearing Loss (NIHL) Claims' by Andrew Mckie, Ian Skeate, Gareth McAloon
'An Introduction to Beauty Negligence Claims – A Practical Guide for the Personal Injury Practitioner' by Greg Almond
'Intercompany Agreements for Transfer Pricing Compliance' by Paul Sutton
'Zen and the Art of Mediation' by Martin Plowman
'A Practical Guide to Adoption for Family Lawyers' by Graham Pegg

'A Practical Guide to Industrial Disease Claims' by Andrew Mckie & Ian Skeate
'A Practical Guide to Conducting a Sheriff Court Proof' by Andrew Stevenson
'A Practical Guide to Vicarious Liability' by Mariel Irvine
'A Practical Guide to Applications for Landlord's Consent and Variation of Leases' by Mark Shelton
'A Practical Guide to Relief from Sanctions Post-Mitchell and Denton' by Peter Causton
'A Practical Guide to Equity Release for Advisors' by Paul Sams
'A Practical Guide to Financial Services Claims' by Chris Hegarty
'A Practical Guide to Financial Ombudsman Service Claims' by Adam Temple & Robert Scrivenor
'A Practical Guide to Running Housing Disrepair and Cavity Wall Claims – Second Edition' by Andrew Mckie & Ian Skeate
'A Practical Guide to Holiday Sickness Claims – Second Edition' by Andrew Mckie & Ian Skeate
'Arguments and Tactics for Personal Injury and Clinical Negligence Claims' by Dorian Williams
'A Practical Guide to Drone Law' by Rufus Ballaster, Andrew Firman, Eleanor Clot
'On Experts: CPR35 for Lawyers and Experts' by David Boyle
'An Introduction to Personal Injury Law' by David Boyle

These books and more are available to order online direct from the publisher at www.lawbriefpublishing.com, where you can also read free sample chapters. For any queries, call us on 0844 587 2383 or email us at mail@lawbriefpublishing.com.

Our books are all generally in stock at www.amazon.co.uk with free next day delivery for Prime members, and at good legal bookshops such as Wildy & Sons.

We are regularly launching new books in our series of practical day-to-day practitioners' guides. Visit our website and join our free newsletter to be kept informed and to receive special offers, free chapters, etc.

You can also follow us on Twitter at www.twitter.com/lawbriefpub.

www.ingramcontent.com/pod-product-compliance
Lightning Source LLC
LaVergne TN
LVHW052318200926
848481LV00002B/598
* 9 7 8 1 9 1 4 6 0 8 4 5 2 *